Praise for
101 Ways to Raise a Happy Baby

"The path to happy self-acceptance begins at birth. This invaluable guide offers parents 101 beautiful ways to help a baby develop a deep-to-the-core sense of joyous self-love that will last a lifetime. Reading it may be the greatest gift you ever give your child."
> —Jack Canfield,
> co-author of *Chicken Soup for the Soul*

"Lisa McCourt's sound and practical advice is a refreshing change from the conventional prescriptions for shaping and controlling your baby's behavior. Following McCourt's invaluable hints will help you rejoice in the unfolding of your child's innate spirit and in your own intuitive capacity to nurture a happy, healthy, and whole baby."
> —Dr. J. Douglas Coatsworth,
> Child and Family Psychologist,
> Center for Family Studies, University of Miami

"What a wonderful, loving and wise approach to parenting! Written in a clear, straightforward, joyful manner, this book empowers parents with the wisdom that's buried deep in their hearts, minds, *and genes* to become the leading experts in raising their own children. You will be forever grateful that you read this well-grounded book. And most importantly, when your happy children are grown, they will thank you for having followed the sage advice contained within these pages."
> —Dr. Daria Wels, Psychologist

continued...

"The strength of Lisa McCourt's words is that she encourages and guides parents to use common sense, love, and intuition. Her creative solutions and obvious love for children can be found on every page."
—Dr. Kathy Levinson,
author of *First Aid for Tantrums*

"This book is a great tool for parents who want to facilitate the process of being happy for their children. A happy, secure, and loved baby will grow into a happy, well-adjusted, and loving adult. A fun, warm, and genuine book!"
—Kathleen Cannon,
children's social worker and play-therapy facilitator

"McCourt writes with great insight into the delicate world of the newborn. Parents will find guidance and support for attachment style parenting."
—Maria Garey,
International Board Certified Lactation Consultant

"Reading this book was like opening my heart. Everyone should raise their children this way!"
—Holly Gallahue,
mother of two and breastfeeding consultant

"An inspiring, fun-to-read book on attachment parenting, and a must for new parents!"
—Abby Zalenski,
mother and childcare provider

"These 101 tips and suggestions are right on the mark! Having a happy baby makes it easy to be a happy mom, and what could be more important than having a happy family?"
—Julie Skokan,
mother of a toddler

101 Ways to Raise a

Happy Baby

Lisa McCourt

LOWELL HOUSE JUVENILE

LOS ANGELES

NTC/Contemporary Publishing Group

Library of Congress Cataloging-in-Publication Data
McCourt, Lisa
    101 ways to raise a happy baby / by Lisa McCourt.
      p.   cm.
    Includes bibliographical reference and index.
    ISBN 0-7373-0270-4
    1. Infants—Care. 2. Infants—Development. 3. Parenting.
    I. Title.   II. Title: One hundred one ways to raise a happy baby.
    III. Title: One hundred and one ways to raise a happy baby.
    RJ61.M483   1999
    649'.122—dc21   99-23464
                                     CIP

Published by Lowell House
A division of NTC/Contemporary Publishing Group, Inc.
4255 West Touhy Avenue, Lincolnwood (Chicago), Illinois 60646-1975 U.S.A.

Lowell House books can be purchased at special discounts when ordered in bulk
for premiums and special sales. Contact Department CS at the following address:
NTC/Contemporary Publishing Group
4255 West Touhy Avenue
Lincolnwood, IL 60646-1975
1-800-323-4900

Roxbury Park is a division of NTC/Contemporary Publishing Group, Inc.

Managing Director and Publisher: Jack Artenstein
Editor in Chief, Roxbury Park Books: Michael Artenstein
Director of Publishing Services: Rena Copperman
Editorial Assistant: Nicole Monastirsky
Cover Design: Mari Saso
Interior Design: Anna Christian
Contributing Illustrator: Cheryl Nathan

Printed and bound in the United States of America
  00 01 DHD 10 9 8 7 6 5 4 3 2

Contents

Acknowledgments

With buckets of thanks to Greg, Cheryl, Abby and Reyna.

There would have been something darkly ironic about making my baby unhappy so I could write a book about happy babies. But thanks to the above four angels, Tuck enjoyed loving companionship during the hours that I spent banging away at this thing, allowing me to be a mommy and a writer simultaneously without compromising little Mr. #1.

Introduction

Your baby is so lucky! Of all the child care books available, you have chosen one to help you raise a HAPPY baby. It was a selfless act, born out of love for that precious new bundle of potentiality that is your child. For the sake of his happiness, you skipped over the books that promised an easy baby, a smarter baby, a confident baby destined for grand achievements, a baby who makes life convenient for his parents. But guess what! Your selflessness has already been rewarded, because raising a happy baby is the best way to get one who's all of those good things.

And raising a truly happy baby is not hard or complicated! It requires only that you strip away the layers of misinformation you have been bombarded with throughout your life so that your own true primal parenting instincts can surface. You already know what your baby needs. You already possess the equipment necessary to communicate with your baby. This book will show you how to get in touch with that amazingly intuitive part of yourself!

I work in children's book publishing, and since kids are my business I've always made a point of learning as much about them as I can. While waiting for my son Tucker to be born, I became fanatical about reading every baby care book and article I could get my hands on. But instead of being comforted by the plethora of information I was accumulating, I found myself utterly confused and distraught. How could best-selling authors and top experts in the field of child rearing be so diametrically opposed on so many crucial issues? It didn't take long to figure out the terrifying truth—*no one really had the answers!*

And why should they? Raising a baby is not a quantifiable science, with laws that can be applied across-the-board or results that can be easily measured with statistics. It's an awe-inspiring, unpredictable, natural, specieswide endeavor! Raising a baby is not an American experience, or a twentieth- or twenty-first-century experience. It's a *human* experience, period. Aside from eating and pooping, it's the most unifying of all human experiences. Why do we as a culture keep applying complicated child-rearing regimens that are as transient as hemlines to an activity that lies at the very core of our humanity? It became increasingly obvious during my investigation that to raise a naturally happy human, parents need only learn how to trust in their babies and in their own human instincts.

During Tucker's first year and a half I added to my treasure trove of research by joining countless mommy organizations and befriending, observing, and grilling a ton of mommies about their parenting practices. This is the result: a collection of tried-and-true happy-baby insights from real moms with a generous sprinkling of quotes from those experts in the field whose concerns are focused where they ought to be—on the true needs of babies.

My best teacher, of course, has been Tucker. His sweet little face is so expressive that he leaves no doubt in my mind as to whether I'm doing the mommy-thing right or not. When I'm not, he graciously offers me the chance to correct my course, and then rewards me with his "That's right! You're getting it!" look. Many pages in this book were written while he slept blissfully in his sling on my chest.

While you read, keep in mind that every single baby is completely unique. When I talk about babies here, I'm talking about the vast majority I've encountered and read about. If what I'm saying does not seem to apply to your baby, LISTEN TO YOUR BABY. Some of my best friends have raised wonderful children by means that contradict many of the Ways offered in this book. They knew what was right for their specific babies and they delivered it.

Your baby will teach you how to take care of her. She's smarter about this being human business than you are because she comes to you with only her humanness, whereas your own humanness is buried beneath layers and layers of stupid stuff that make up our society's here-today-gone-tomorrow views on child rearing. Don't subscribe to trendy information when doing something as monumental and timeless as raising your baby. Look inside, trust your heart, and read on!

How to Use This Book

Read these Ways from start to finish for a chronological tour through baby's first eighteen months, or use this alphabetical subject guide to help you find answers to your questions. (The index will help you locate even more specific information.)

Bathing time

Bedtime

Bonding with baby

Bottlefeeding

Breastfeeding

Carrying baby

Communication

Dressing baby

Eating

Equipment

Rocking

Schedules

Self-esteem

Sharing activities

Substitute caregivers

Toddlers

Touching

Travel

1.

Get attached!

A happy baby is a bonded baby. It sounds kind of mystical, this bonding thing—almost like a phenomenon to be believed in or not. And there's certainly no guarantee that you will pop out a baby you will instantly be willing to lay down your life for. In fact, the big love—I mean the big, big, love that gives you goosebumps and makes your eyes well up and your breath catch in your throat—doesn't always happen in the first few days or even weeks. For some parents it does, but for many others, true, intense bonding takes time.

Bonding is falling in love—and just like in adult love, it deepens with every tender moment of shared contact, every sweet whispered word, every adoring gaze. Quite simply, the more time baby spends in your affectionate embrace, the more bonded he will become, the more bonded YOU will become, and the more relaxed and happy you both will feel.

While researching the experts' advice on baby care, I found that one style of parenting stood out above all others in facilitating bonding, and therefore, in promoting happiness in babies. Dr. William Sears (far and away my favorite expert) calls it "attachment parenting," and I'm going to borrow his phrase for this parenting plan, which is really not a plan at all. It's simply the way the human animal happily raises its offspring when left to its own innate wisdom.

The most important thing you can do to raise a happy baby is to listen to her and fully believe that you instinctively understand what's best for her! Your most basic instincts are in perfect sync with your baby's. Your baby is born knowing that you should hold, caress, and love her and go out of your way to meet her needs. Your instincts are to do all of these things. The only obstacle is the barrage of "up-to-date" advice bombarding you!

There are many opposing theories out there regarding how babies should be treated. And American moms are left without any tradition to fall back on, because every few years the experts change and so do the dictates. How are we to ever trust our instincts with this steady flow of heavy-handed and forever changing advice? The truth is, there is not a book in the world you can buy that will tell you the correct way to raise your own baby. You alone are meant to work out that one-of-a-kind puzzle, and only one person has the answer key: your baby! The whole trick is to *know* your baby so that *your baby* can teach you how to raise him happily.

And that is where attachment parenting comes in, since its basic tenets are the building blocks of the big BOND. Attached parents respond immediately to their babies' cues. They carry their babies, breastfeed, and sleep with their babies. Though it is possible to bond with your child without subscribing to all of these practices, they do provide the optimum matrix for bonding and therefore for promoting happiness.

For a human being of any age to be happy, she has to feel a sense of her own goodness and rightness in her environment. She needs a strong sense of self-esteem, and she needs to feel understood and valued. Happy babies communicate their needs easily because they are closely bonded to their parents, and that bond is what this book is all about.

2.

How will you feed your baby? Do the research!

With so much to gain by breastfeeding, it is surprising that the majority of American mothers still end up bottlefeeding their babies. If you are pregnant and planning to bottlefeed, you owe it to yourself and to your baby to do as much research as you can on the benefits of breastfeeding before making your final choice.

I have one friend who was told by hospital nurses that her baby "preferred the bottle." She wanted the best for her baby so she gave up breastfeeding and has regretted her decision ever since.

Sometimes a new mother feels pressured to follow the lead of family matriarchs who bottlefed their babies. These women were being the best mothers they could be according to the information they were given at the time. Explain to them that much more is known today about the tremendous health advantages and psychological advantages of breastfeeding.

Many women who bottlefeed their babies claim that they had wanted to breastfeed but were unable to for various reasons. However, according to M. Sara Rosenthal, author of *The Pregnancy Sourcebook,* "It is crucial to note that only about 1 percent of all mothers are biologically incapable of producing enough breast milk for their newborns."

More likely, these women had very common breastfeeding difficulties and would have succeeded with a little perseverance. Reknown childcare expert Penelope Leach writes in *Your Baby and Child,* "Almost all women, including many who try to nurse but succumb to painful breast problems or the tyranny of the baby scales, would have been able to breastfeed if they had had enough self-confidence, support from partners and others (especially mothers), and skilled, sensitive professional help on demand."

If you want to breastfeed, rest assured that chances are, you *will* be able to. Attend La Leche League meetings while you are pregnant and buy or borrow a copy of the group's book, *The Womanly Art of Breastfeeding.* There are scads of other good books about nursing, and your hospital probably offers a breastfeeding class you can take before you deliver.

Pack the numbers of La Leche League leaders and lactation consultants in your hospital bag so that you can get whatever help you need right away. Be emphatically clear with all hospital staff that you intend to nurse your child and absolutely no bottles are to be given.

If you begin breastfeeding and later change your mind, a switch to bottlefeeding is easy. But if you begin by bottlefeeding, your body will stop producing milk and you could forever lose your opportunity to breastfeed.

3.

Go to La Leche League meetings.

I want to dispel the La Leche League myth. I don't know how this came to be, but it seems that when many otherwise well-informed people hear the words *La Leche League,* they picture a coven of half-naked gypsies sitting around breastfeeding their eight-year-olds while discussing natural resource conservation and munching on tofu squares. In my friend Kenny's colorful imagination, these "militant boob-pushers" hypnotize new moms to initiate them into the cult, and then force them into years of breastfeeding slavery.

Kenny, dear, it just isn't so. The women I've encountered through La Leche League have been fun, intelligent, sophisticated women who happen to nurse their babies. They offer one another invaluable insights at their monthly meetings, and La Leche League leaders have the answers to absolutely any question on breastfeeding. Pregnant women are welcome, as well as those undecided about nursing, and contrary to popular belief, moms who are leaning toward the bottle are not tarred and feathered upon entry. To find the league meetings and leaders nearest you, call 1-800-525-3243.

You can call a league leader anytime, with any question, even if you've never attended a meeting. These amazing women volunteer for the job. No one pays them; they just truly want to help you nurse your baby. When Tucker was born I had the numbers of three different women so I wouldn't have to bother any one too frequently, and I was never rushed off the phone by any of them—no matter how inane my question.

Take advantage of this very valuable FREE resource!

4.

Feed your baby's body and soul.

Your baby is born with a limited vocabulary, and you, too, have a limited vocabulary for truly communicating with him. Your most effective communication tools are those two now-mountainous orbs of flesh on your chest. Whatever your relationship with them has been in the past, it's time to renegotiate the contract. This is what they've been waiting for all your life!

Unless you've been stuck in a black hole somewhere, you know that breastfeeding is the healthiest thing you can do for your baby. But it is also one of the best ways to have a *happy* baby. Your baby won't enter this world with a lot of hobbies—nursing will be his first and most pressing desire. Nursing is every bit as psychologically nourishing as it is physically nourishing. When you put your baby to your breast, you are communicating the message "I'm your mommy. I'm here. I want to meet your needs."

Breastfeeding makes baby happy not only from the pleasure of enjoying her naturally favorite activity but also from the closeness and skin contact she gets with you, from the bonding-facilitating hormones that are released in both you and her, and even from the taste. Try a little taste of your own expressed breast milk (sweet!) and then formula (nasty!) and you will understand baby's preference.

But maybe you are one of those women who finds the mere idea of some little creature suckling at your breast distasteful. Many of my nursing friends felt that way before meeting their babies. My suggestion is, just try it! If you give it a fair chance and truly hate it, stop. Happy babies do not coexist with unhappy, resentful mommies.

Keep in mind that your first nursing experiences are going to be your worst and that the longer you do it, the more you'll like it. It's true that breastfeeding is extremely time-consuming for the first few weeks, but is that really so bad? What a great excuse to spend lots of time relaxing with your baby and delegating everything else that needs to get done! After the first month, the whole procedure becomes much less draining (no pun intended) and more rewarding, and it *does* keep getting better after that.

Plus, maybe you'll like it more than you think. Breastfeeding isn't the ultimate give-a-thon those smug, self-sacrificing mommies make it look like. There are plenty of selfish reasons to give it a try. The most obvious is that you don't have to buy and measure and prepare and tote around stinky old formula that stains the Baby Gaps and makes diapers and spit-up smell and look all cottage-cheesy-awful. (Breastfed babies' poop doesn't smell! Honest!)

Then, there's the calorie-sucker benefit: breastfeeding babies conveniently suck the calories out of you so that you can dwindle back to your prepregnancy shape faster than your size-larger clothes go out of style.

If that's not enough to convince you, think about how much money you'll save not having to buy formula and also about how women who breastfeed have a lower incidence of breast cancer. Not to mention how much healthier breastfed babies are, resulting in less discomfort for baby, fewer trips to the doctor, and fewer medical bills.

In the early months, when baby truly loves so little else, watching your newborn angel nurse is as good as it gets. The feel of that sweet breath and that unbelievably soft cheek against your skin, the sound of gentle sucking, and that tiny, trusting hand patting you lovingly . . . this is the stuff mothering memories are made of.

5.

Bottlefeed with warm, loving contact.

If you do your research and make the decision that bottlefeeding is the only acceptable course for you, resolve to be happy about it! Skip over sections in this or any other book that extol the virtues of breastfeeding, and don't start driving yourself crazy with guilt or remorse. Your baby needs you to be happily confident in your care for him, and studies have proven that lots of loving contact is more important for baby's psychological well-being than nursing itself is.

You don't have to be intimidated by mommy-snobbies who question your mothering in this area. You don't owe anyone an explanation. Borrow my friend Jennifer's response to any impolite inquiries into her daughter's nourishment: With a big smile and a tone of voice that clearly puts an end to the conversation, she says, "Yes, Lindsay's bottlefed and she's just fine."

While it is true that breastfeeding facilitates bonding, you can do a lot to replicate the breastfeeding experience when you give your baby a bottle. If you're at home, try partially undressing yourself and the baby for optimum skin-to-skin contact. Position the bottle close to your breast and maintain loving eye contact with baby while he sucks. Caress and kiss and cuddle him in a soothing, nonstimulating manner.

Dr. William Sears suggests, "You want your baby to feel that the bottle is part of you. Most babies, breastfed and bottlefed, feed better if you are quiet while they suck, but babies enjoy social interaction during pauses in the feedings. Watch your baby for signals that he wants to socialize during the feeding. Eventually you will develop an intuitive sense of your baby's feeding rhythm. Baby should feel that a person is feeding him, not just a bottle."

Other tips Dr. Sears offers bottlefeeding moms include feeding baby on request instead of by a strict schedule, being responsive to baby's signals, and never forcing baby to finish a bottle if he shows signs that he's full.

6.

Pick him up!

In recent decades, Western culture has accepted a bizarre notion that crying alone is somehow good for a baby. No primitive society has ever shared this unnatural opinion and neither do most contemporary cultures.

In fact, most other societies recognize a transition phase during which mother-baby contact is essential. It is believed that nine months inside the womb and nine months of intensive mothering outside the womb are required to adequately prepare a human infant to spend any time alone.

The necessary components of the second-nine-month-transition phase are close mother-baby contact, prompt response to crying, and breastfeeding until at least the age of two. As radical as all this may sound, it is commonplace outside of Western culture. Anthropologists repeatedly report that one of the most striking differences between babies in the Western world and those in the preliterate world is that in the latter, babies seldom cry, and if they do, they are usually picked up immediately and nursed or soothed in some other way.

Many experts are now telling us what we mothers have always known in our hearts. Babies should not be left to cry alone. According to renown child care expert Lee Salk, picking up a baby when she cries teaches her that someone responds to her needs, whether those needs are for food or merely for the physical sensation of being held. He tells parents, "There is no harm in a child crying; the harm is done if his cries are not answered."

Most parents will try to determine the reason for baby's crying so they can fix it. But very often, there is no apparent reason, and that is perfectly normal and appropriate. Babies sometimes just feel bad and long for human contact and love. If parents comfort baby when they believe she has a legitimate reason for crying, but ignore her when they don't believe she does, they are teaching her that people are not to be trusted. She will feel confused and powerless and not worth their attention.

Crying is the only way a baby can communicate! When cries go unanswered often enough, the baby will come to think she is an ineffective communicator. Once that belief is established in infancy, it is likely to become fulfilled in later childhood.

In nature, almost all mammal mothers respond immediately to their babies' cries. The mothers nurse, lick, or touch their young as an automatic response to any discomfort they sense in them.

Even human children, when left to their own instincts, will rush to help a crying baby. Don't let the ridiculous advice of some recent "expert" get in the way of your own biological imperative to pick up and nurture your child.

7.

Ditch the schedule!

In Buddhism, there is a maxim that describes one aspect of perfect Buddha nature. It says, "Eat when hungry; sleep when tired." How simple that is, and yet how complicated we make life for our babies when we attempt to rob them of this most natural human right. Babies are not meant to follow schedules. Their tremendous rate of growth is far from steady in the first eighteen months—it proceeds unpredictably, in spurts. That means that babies' needs for food and for rest are highly variable. The only way to make sure they get the right amount of both is to tune into their cues and trust them to call the shots.

If a baby is fed (breast or bottle) according to a schedule instead of when she cries to alert her caregiver that she's hungry, she will get the message that her hunger cues are wrong and she'll come to distrust them. Similarly, if a parent forces a rigid sleeping schedule on a baby, the baby will learn to disregard her natural feelings of tiredness. Causing a baby to distrust her own internal cues does her a terrible disservice.

If babies are allowed to follow their natural desires to eat when they're hungry and stop when they're full, such patterns will become second nature to them. They'll be much less likely to develop eating disorders later in life. And if baby is encouraged to sleep only when he's tired, he'll sleep better and be less likely to develop sleep disturbances.

Experts who advise schedules for babies are often popular with parents who are looking for shortcuts. A scheduled baby would seem to be an easy baby. But when you take into account all the tears and frustrations (both babies' and parents') spent in trying to bend baby's will to make him conform to the arbitrary schedule, you will find that a much easier route is just to listen to baby and respond to his needs.

In Japan, as well as in most traditional cultures, there is no concept of bedtimes for babies. The babies remain with the parents until sleepy, and then they fall asleep wherever they are. There is no crying, no struggle, no abandonment. When the parents themselves are ready to go to bed, they pick up their sleeping children and take them to bed with them. Sleep problems are almost nonexistent in Japanese children.

Not having to overcome painful separation from their parents, these babies don't suck their thumbs to self-soothe; they don't become attached to transitional objects like teddy bears or blankets; they don't make their parents get up repeatedly throughout the night.

Of course, schedules are only bad when they're imposed on a baby. Many babies fall into amazingly regular schedules on their own. If that's the case with your baby, enjoy the predictability, but don't be surprised if she revises the plan from time to time.

8.

Start making baby happy while you are still pregnant.

Amazingly, research indicates that your stress level while you are pregnant may contribute to your baby's general level of stress. Noted pediatrician T. Berry Brazelton conducted a study comparing the lifestyles of three different groups of Japanese women while they were pregnant, and then comparing the attributes of their newborn babies. The women who lived a low-key, country lifestyle on Japan's Goto Islands had babies who were notably calmer and had longer attention spans than the babies of the women in Tokyo, who lived a more fast-paced, urban lifestyle. The third group, the Japanese women living in San Francisco, had the most frantic lifestyles of all, and correspondingly, their babies were the jumpiest, most agitated, and had the shortest attention spans.

Music researcher Don Campbell writes in *The Mozart Effect*:

> I believe a mother's strong emotions—from anger and resentment to deep calm, gratitude, and acceptance—can create hormonal changes and neurological impulses that affect the fetus. In many traditional societies, it has long been recognized that all the influences to which the growing baby is exposed contribute to its health and well-being. In Japan, Tai-kyo, or embryonic education, was, until the early part of the twentieth century, a part of how families prepared for newborns. The voices, thoughts, and feelings of the mother and father, grandparents, and other family members were believed to influence the fetus, and disharmonious vibrations of all kinds were avoided. Today that would include blaring television sets, violent films, loud music, and other sounds that might upset a growing baby.

In his amazing book, *The Secret Life of the Unborn Child,* Dr. Thomas Verny describes how Boris Brott, the conductor of the Hamilton Philharmonic Orchestra in Ontario, Canada, was puzzled by a mysterious ability to play certain pieces brilliantly by ear, while he struggled to master all other pieces. The answer came when he learned that while she was pregnant, his mother had played those selections that came so effortlessly to him. Embryologists agree that the ear is the first organ to develop in the embryo, becoming functional after just eighteen weeks and capable of active listening from twenty-four weeks on.

In a landmark study at the University of North Carolina, Dr. Tony DeCasper and Dr. Melanie Spence instructed pregnant women to read Dr. Seuss's *The Cat in the Hat* to their bellies during the third trimester of their pregnancies. The newborn babies demonstrated through sucking tests that they could recognize verses from the book and distinguish them from other reading material!

Researchers now know that an unborn baby is sensitive not only to music and sounds, but also to the emotion in his mother's voice and possibly even the meaning of her words. Take advantage of this remarkable opportunity to get a headstart on bonding. Pay attention to what your baby hears while you are pregnant. Make up songs just for the baby and sing them lovingly when you're alone in the house or car. Don't feel silly. Even if you don't believe your baby understands what you're singing, it will get you in a great frame of mind for bonding with your little guest when he arrives. And give Dad and other friends and relatives a chance too!

9.

Rock-a-bye your baby.

All over the world parents comfort their babies by rocking them. Without consciously knowing why, they rock at a rate of sixty to seventy rocks per minute. Babies respond so well to this rate of rocking because it reminds them of the womb! Mom's resting heartbeat was set to the same rhythm, and so was her gait at the end of her pregnancy.

Babies need movement. Those who aren't carried or rocked enough will flail their limbs and clench and unclench their fists, trying to provide a little motion for themselves. With or without an official rocking chair, when we rock babies we help them develop a sense of balance, which is the first step to learning body control.

Don't depend on a cradle! To get the full benefits of rocking, babies need to be held upright. Studies have shown that most parents instinctively hold babies with their left arms, on the left sides of their bodies. Our instincts seem to be telling us that babies prefer that side, and in fact, they do. Your baby can feel your heartbeat there; your left arm is warmer than your right since it's closer to your heart; and having baby's right side pressed against you actually helps his digestive functioning!

Plus, since the left side of the body is controlled by the right side of the brain (the emotional side), it has even been speculated that the left side of the face is more expressive than the right. By holding babies in the way that feels most natural to us, we are actually showing babies our more tender, emotive side, and perhaps our left eye and ear are even more receptive to baby's emotional cues!

Mothering magazine cites a study that demonstrated how rocking baby in a rocking chair helped mothers get over C-sections. The group that rocked had less pain, less intestinal gas, and also walked and left the hospital sooner. Women in the same study who gave birth vaginally found that rocking relaxed their abdominal muscles while promoting better digestion, appetite, and blood circulation.

Why resist doing something that feels so good to baby and so good to mommy too? I love this beautiful description from *Mothering*: "When babies sleep, they snuggle tight into your shoulder. Their warm, milky scent tickles your nose, the ultimate aromatherapy. Tension is pulled from your body like the moon pulls the tides out to sea—naturally, inexorably. The motion of the rocking chair offers a comforting solution to all the day's problems. A soothing touch by another person, in fact, has been shown to slow the human heartbeat. Swaying back and forth with your tiny tranquilizer erases everything but the satisfaction of the moment."

Race you to the rocker!

10.

Don't be a closet nurser.

Breastfeeding in public is more accepted than it has ever been, but we still have a long way to go! Help the cause by proudly feeding your baby whenever and wherever necessary. It is utterly ridiculous that mothers in our society should be made to feel ashamed or embarrassed for doing the most natural and loving thing we humans are equipped to do. Baby will be happiest if she's given the opportunity to nurse as her needs arise as long as she senses that Mom is happy and comfortable meeting those needs.

Once you've gotten the hang of breastfeeding at home, sit in front of a mirror and practice more discreet positions for your public debut. Then take your show on the road! When you're confident with public breastfeeding, you can freely go anywhere with your precious parcel, making life-with-baby much more closely resemble life-before-baby.

One of the best resources I've discovered for shy-about-nursing moms is Motherwear catalog. (Call 1-800-950-2500 to get one.) You can order attractive clothes with discreet nursing openings that make it incredibly easy to feed your baby anywhere without anyone peeping at so much as a centimeter of your breast.

One warning: While their shirts run pretty true to size, their dresses run really, really big (probably to make us new moms feel better). I'm normally a solid size six but I have to order dresses from

Motherwear in extra-small and then have them taken in. Thankfully, they have the most liberal return policy in the world, encouraging you to exchange clothes you've worn and even washed if you decide you ordered the wrong size. The clothes are a little pricey, but they're made of heavy-duty cotton for lots of washings, and the patterns are especially designed to camouflage spit-up and baby-drool spots. It's worth the investment to build a small wardrobe of staples from this catalog because as easy as it is to just lift up a shirt, there are some circumstances that call for an almost invisible way to nurse.

11.

Use all of your heightened senses to bond with baby.

Studies have shown that newborn babies can identify their mothers by smell! When researchers placed a breast pad damp with a mother's milk on one side of her newborn's head and another woman's milk on the other side, the babies turned toward their own mother's milk 80 percent of the time. And while you may not believe it, you have similar amazing abilities! After just a few days, most mothers can distinguish *by smell* clothing worn by their own babies from clothing worn by other babies.

Even more remarkable is how quickly our sense of touch can bond us to our babies. About 70 percent of blindfolded mothers who spent at least an hour with their infants following birth are able to pick their babies out of a lineup just by the feel of their hands or cheeks. Dads are amazingly good at this too!

Dr. T. Berry Brazelton shows mothers how important they are to their infants by demonstrating that babies know and prefer their mothers' voices. He asks the mom to softly say baby's name in one ear while he does the same in the baby's other ear. Without fail, the babies turn toward their mothers. Similarly, mothers can usually distinguish their own babies' cries from those of other babies of the same age.

Numerous studies have been done which show that, when given a choice, babies will choose to look at a human face over any other image. And by just two days old, infants will choose their mother's face over any other. Though still legally blind, they are programmed to focus on an image approximately 8 to 12 inches in front of them—the precise distance between a mother and her nursing infant. And no one has to remind a new parent how mesmerizing it is to gaze into the face of his or her own newborn child.

So while you're getting to know your scrumptious new charge, keep in mind that all of your senses are heightened by the human miracle you have just taken part in. Nature has given you a temporary magical gift—use it to bond with your baby in every possible way.

12.

Recognize the limitations of your pediatrician.

Your baby's pediatrician is a highly trained *medical* professional. But when it comes to parenting issues, she is just another parent, if in fact she even is a parent. Questions like "Where should my baby sleep?" and "How much should I hold my baby?" and "How long should I let my baby cry?" are not medical questions, so your pediatrician's answer to those questions should hold no more weight than your dry cleaner's response.

Most doctors hate such questions anyway. The most professional answer they can give is something to the effect of "Whatever works best for your family is fine with me. I will support your parenting decisions as long as they don't conflict with your child's medical needs." When doctors give more specific advice than this, be fully aware that you are being offered an *opinion* that has little if anything at all to do with pediatric credentials.

That said, there's nothing wrong with interviewing pediatricians to find one who supports your parenting philosophies. It's hard not to view each well-visit as a report card on your mothering, though we all know we're not supposed to feel that way. I personally love being praised for my parenting choices by Tucker's pediatrician (who was selected, in part, because I knew he was an attachment-parenting advocate)!

Whatever you do, don't let parenting advice from a doctor or anyone else override your own maternal instincts. When wrestling with any parenting dilemma, the most important entities to consult are your own heart and your own baby.

13.

Keep baby close.

Unfortunately, ours is a culture that routinely separates mothers and babies for much of the time. We leave babies in plastic carriers, strollers, playpens, or at day care centers, and even when we are at home with our babies and could be touching them, we are sometimes advised to let babies cry and suffer alone.

This lifestyle places a tremendous amount of stress on babies, but luckily, the tide is turning and much evidence is surfacing to make baby holding the norm. Did you know that breastfeeding in our country was on the brink of extinction until the 1960s when enough research finally proved that Mother Nature had the superior recipe? It's hard to imagine that we believed the formula manufacturers who tried to convince us otherwise! Similarly, sufficient research has now finally proved that giving babies enough touch is as necessary as giving them enough food.

Australian psychoanalyst Dr. Peter Cook writes, "I suggest that child rearing in English-speaking societies is emerging from an era in which many widely held beliefs, values, attitudes, and practices have been so out of harmony with the genetically influenced nature and needs of mothers and their developing children, that they have contributed to conflict, stress, and emotional and behavioral disturbances in the infant and developing child."

He explains our problem is that we don't trust our children. We've invented this notion that children are selfish, manipulative, tyrannical little things who are out to enslave us instead of recognizing the simple truth that they are naturally dependent on us to meet their needs. We set up children as the adversaries at exactly the time when we desperately need to be forging cooperative, loving connections.

Your baby needs your touch A LOT. Ashley Montagu, Ph.D, says in *Touching,* "The manner in which the young of all mammals snuggle and cuddle against the body of the mother and against the bodies of their siblings or of any other introduced animal strongly suggests that cutaneous stimulation is an important biological need, for both their physical and their behavioral development."

It is a ridiculous, yet sadly prevalent, notion that babies can be harmed by too much holding. All the latest research proves nothing could be farther from the truth. Babies have serious physical and emotional needs. Meet them! A held baby gets to view things the way you see them, affording her an invaluable opportunity to peek at how the world works. Even at this early stage, baby is learning about the culture she will someday inhabit.

Carrying a baby all the time is an acquired skill but one well worth developing! Babies are heavy to lug around initially, but the strangely magical truth is that even though they keep increasing in weight, they get easier and easier to carry. Part of this phenomenon is due to the fact that at about four months old baby starts helping by holding onto you and keeping her back straight while she straddles your hip. The other part is that if you are an accustomed baby-carrier, you will get stronger faster than your baby gets heavier. Baby becomes your personal trainer, increasing your resistance in tiny increments just as you are ready for it to create your own personalized weight-lifting program.

The easiest way by far to get on a frequent-carry program is to sling your baby. He'll love it! Read on for all the reasons you'll love it too.

14.

Strap baby on!

Babies who are worn in slings are happy babies. This falls under the category of listening to your baby and believing in her wisdom. Your baby does not want to be left alone in a crib or carrier while you go about your day. Baby's cries are to alert you to this message. Yet carrying baby in your arms for much of the time would likely leave you exhausted and unproductive. The answer is the baby sling. This piece of equipment should be the very first item on your inventory list. I cannot stress enough the degree to which it will enhance your life—and your baby's.

Babies have been worn in slings in cultures other than our own for centuries. Why? Because they provide the ultimate win-win situation for parents as well as their offspring. Once you get used to "wearing" your baby, you will be amazed to find that you can do almost all the things you did before baby's arrival. But convenience for you is just one of the many reasons to practice this time-honored custom.

Being born thrusts a baby into an unfamiliar and potentially terrifying set of circumstances. The best way to relieve this postnatal stress and to help ease the transition is to make things as familiar for baby as possible. In a sling, a baby can curl comfortably into the fetal tuck; he can hear Mommy's heartbeat and her voice, feel her breathing and her warmth, and enjoy the rhythm of her walk. Is it any wonder babies thrive under such conditions and dislike being left all alone in a crib or carrier? We have discussed the theory that a human's gestation period should be thought of as eighteen months: nine months in and nine months out. Babywearing is the solution for that second nine-month period.

Babywearing actually helps babies regulate their bodily systems, know nighttime from daytime, develop a sense of balance, and stay healthy. Dr. William Sears explains:

> Fussing and disorganized behavior is a withdrawal symptom—a result of the loss of the regulatory effects of the attachment to the mother. Babies should not be left alone to self-soothe, as some parenting advisers suggest. This style of detached parenting is not supported by common sense, experience, or research. Behavioral research has repeatedly shown that infants exhibit more anxious and disorganized behaviors when separated from their mothers. While there is a variety of child-rearing theories, attachment researchers all agree on one thing: In order for a baby's emotional, intellectual, and physiological systems to function optimally, the continued presence of the mother, as during babywearing, is a necessary regulatory influence.

Babywearing makes breastfeeding easy to do anywhere, but it's especially important for bottlefed babies. Studies have shown that the continuous contact provided by using a sling is even more beneficial to the bonding process than breastfeeding is. Babies have excess energy they are not able to discharge on their own. A baby releases this energy through her caregiver, by participating in the sling wearer's walking, talking, laughing, working, and playing. This is the framework in which bonding takes place, no matter how baby is fed.

15.

Choose the best sling for you, and then practice!

People stop me constantly when I'm out with Tuck to say, "Where did you get that? It looks so comfortable!" Most of the baby carriers currently available in stores are not true slings. They strap baby to your body in confining and often unnatural positions. They distribute baby's weight unevenly and put a tremendous strain on the wearer's neck, shoulder, and back muscles. They end up in the bottom of the closet and baby ends up in the stroller. But all my mommy-friends who use real slings are ardent devotees who never go anywhere without them. So here's a rundown on the best baby slings and how to get them.

My absolute favorite is the Over the Shoulder Baby Holder (OTSBH). It's unbelievably comfortable and comes in really nice fabrics. (We get the most compliments on our tie-dye sling!) Its two-ring design adjusts easily to fit a variety of wearers, although it comes in sizes for added assurance of a perfect fit. The padding and even distribution of baby's weight contribute to its all-day comfort, and it works for newborns up to four-year-olds. It's available through people who act as distributors for the manufacturer. Call 1-800-637-9246 to locate the nearest one.

One sling that's easy to find in baby stores is similar to the OTSBH. It's made by Nojo and called The Original Baby Sling. If you are a tall person, you may like it just as much as the OTSBH, though the fabric selection is much more limited. However, if you are of average height or shorter, you may find that the one-size Nojo holds your baby too low and too loosely for ultimate comfort. At the same time, it has less fabric for expansion as your baby grows.

If you'll be considering your slings fashion accessories (like I do!) look into getting a Maya Wrap. The Maya Wrap has a design similar to that of the OTSBH and The Original Baby Sling but is less comfortable because it lacks padding. The lack of padding does give it a more sophisticated look, however, and the fabrics are very beautiful. I use mine as a "dress" sling, when I want to wear Tuck to business meetings or to fancy shindigs.

Maya Wrap offers a second design that is even easier to put on than the above-mentioned sling. It has no feature for adjusting the fit, but you can buy it in sizes. There are no rings to this design. You simply slip it over your shoulder and drop baby in. Again, the lack of padding makes it less comfortable than some, but it may be right for you if you find the ring-style sling too complicated. Order Maya Wrap slings by calling 1-888-MAYAWRAP.

A slightly more comfortable sling with the same design as this second Maya Wrap is the New Native Baby Carrier (1-800-646-1682). I love the organically grown cotton version, and the deep pouch holds baby securely. But the baby hangs too low in this sling for me, even in the smallest size (and I'm 5'6"). The directions include instructions for sewing a temporary seam to make it smaller. That sounds fine in theory, but I'm just not equipped—machinery- or patience-wise—to start altering this thing. My very tall husband uses it when he exercises on his stationary bike with Tuck, and he claims it's comfortable. But being used to the padding in the OTSBH, I find that all the unpadded slings hurt my shoulder after a while.

The most important thing to remember with any sling is that it's going to feel weird at first. So many moms tell me, "I bought one of those but couldn't get the hang of it," or "It wasn't comfortable for me." Wearing a sling seldom feels completely natural right away. And wearers often make the mistake of trying it for the first time when they're out somewhere and baby is already fussing.

Practice with your sling around the house for a few days before you venture out with it. Try all the different positions and always be sure the bottom of the sling crosses *low* on your back. Baby will cooperate best if you start walking around as soon as he is in the sling. The slings all come with instructions, and *The Baby Book* by William and Martha Sears has an excellent babywearing section with illustrations of the different holds. (That book, by the way, is the absolute best all-around baby care book you can buy.) Trust me—the initial awkwardness will soon go away and you won't believe you ever lived without this invaluable device!

16.

Let baby sleep where he's happiest.

While some authorities still advise against it, many developmental psychologists and more and more childcare experts are endorsing a family bed. Since the Stone Age, babies have slept next to their mothers, and co-sleeping was common to all human cultures up until a tiny blip ago in the grand scheme of human evolution.

The custom of infants sleeping apart from their mothers is regional and recent, and as all parents know, most babies have a very hard time adjusting to it. The most well-known current proponent of forcing babies to sleep alone is a doctor whose popular sleep-training regimen involves leaving babies isolated in their cribs to cry themselves to sleep.

While acknowledging that baby will violently protest the situation, this doctor insists parents never give in to their instincts to take baby to their bed. His instructions are to leave baby in his crib no matter how much he cries and to let him cry for longer and longer periods before comforting him—until baby eventually learns that his cries will not get a response and he begins to sleep alone without excessive crying.

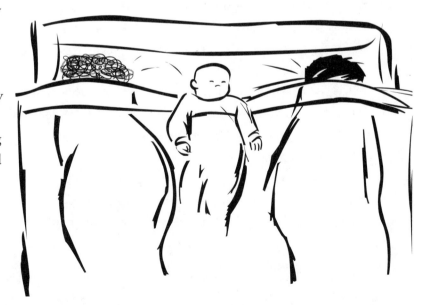

This doctor's book gained popularity because it delivered what it promised: babies who ultimately stopped bothering their parents at night. But parents would never have embraced his technique if he hadn't repeatedly assured them that this sleep-training regimen was in the best interest of the child. Though I'm sure the doctor believed that it was, many researchers have proved the opposite—that such deprivation of nighttime nurturing is harmful to baby's emerging sense of self.

Childcare specialist Tine Thevenin writes, "A child who has been forced to accept, after nights of terrified screaming, that her parents will not come to her rescue, will seem to give up and accept her condition. One cannot but wonder, however, what lasting effect this feeling of abandonment, this rage, this fear will have on her for the rest of her life. It is a powerful experience to call for another human being and be ignored."

She points out that throughout the ages, shunning has been used as the severest form of punishment in many cultures, including the societies of Australian aborigines, ancient Roman citizens, Amish farmers, and West Point cadets. According to Mihaly Csikszentmihalyi, former chairman of the psychology department at the University of Chicago, "often, the worst sanction the community can issue is shunning. The person ignored grows gradually depressed, and soon begins to doubt his or her very existence. . . . We are biologically programmed to find other human beings the most important objects in the world." Imagine how powerful that effect can be on an infant who has barely a grasp on her distinct existence to begin with!

If you are ever tempted to let your baby "cry it out" please buy and read *Nighttime Parenting,* by Dr. William Sears. He sensitively and humanely offers sound advice for getting baby to sleep without subjecting her to psychological damage that could possibly last a lifetime.

My friend Julie began the co-sleeping habit accidentally the night her baby, Luke, was born. Still in the hospital, recovering from a C-section, she was nursing Luke in the middle of the night when Luke, she, and her husband all fell asleep. (Luke's dad was supposed to return Luke to his bassinet after the feeding.) The nurse reprimanded the peacefully sleeping family when she found them, but Julie knew from that moment on that this was how she and Luke were meant to spend their nighttime hours. Her word for sleeping next to Luke was *heaven.*

Luke is a secure, mellow, charming toddler now, and Julie couldn't be more pleased with their ongoing family bed experience. She writes in Luke's baby book, "Falling asleep and waking up times are special for Daddy too. He travels and works long hours so his contact with Luke at bedtime, at night, and first thing in the morning really helps them connect and feel close to each other. Having Luke near me helps me be a better mom because I can comfort him before he wakes up from restless sleep.

He doesn't ever cry to signal he's awake. He saves cries for when he's hurting from a bad fall or from an illness. The family bed has definitely helped Luke be a happier baby."

Ultimately, of course, it is up to each family to decide what works best for them. I've heard that some babies actually prefer to sleep alone, and if that is the case with your child, you will do him no harm by honoring his preference. Or, some parents may feel very strongly that they will not adjust happily to sharing their bed. In such a case, the baby is better off alone than he would be sleeping with resentful parents.

On the subject of family beds, Penelope Leach says:

> Sharing a family bed will not stop your baby from waking up and it will not save you from night feedings in the first weeks. But if he is sharing your bed with you, your baby's awakenings and his feeding will disturb you far less than they will if you have to go to him. And, because he is where he best likes to be—close against you—he will go back to sleep far more quickly and easily. Babies who sleep in family beds from early on often wake much less than other babies as they get older. As they get older still, they may wake but find it unnecessary to wake you. After all, a toddler who is with you in bed does not need to cry for a cuddle because he is already having it or can just snuggle up.

17.

If you must crib-train your baby, do it lovingly.

Crib-training is the ritual whereby parents force a baby to accept that he will have to sleep alone in a crib in a room apart from his parents. Different experts prescribe different routines, but most involve leaving the child to cry alone for a specified time until he eventually gives up and accepts his fate.

A mother might assume that because she leaves her child to cry alone for only a short period of time, no harm can be done, but we must remember that babies have no sense of time. The abandonment a baby feels during any given moment is every bit as real as it would be if her mother had left her, alone and unable to care for herself, forever.

If you are absolutely deadset against welcoming your baby into your bed or at least your room, Penelope Leach's crib-training approach is the one that seems the most humane to me. Your baby will most likely cry when left alone in a crib, since it goes against his nature, but leaving him alone to cry is not your only option.

Leach suggests going to your baby immediately every time he cries. Do not take baby out of the crib and do not play with baby, but do touch and comfort and talk to baby until he stops crying. If you are a nursing mom, baby will probably accept this routine better from Dad than he will from you. It will be exhausting work for a while, but eventually baby will learn that his cries will not get him out of the crib. However, he will be spared the other lesson that often inadvertently goes hand-in-hand with crib training, that he is not valuable and his parents are unconcerned about his discomfort and fear. (See Way 59 for information on the *Baby-Go-to-Sleep* tapes.)

Be aware that even with the most severe methods, many babies simply will not comply. These determined babies never give up the hope that you will come for them if they signal you enough. If you have one of these children, please surrender the fight and listen to your heart. Somehow, this baby remains certain that he is worth your time and attention—don't let him down!

18.

Respect the reflex.

Infants can't control their limbs. This annoys them to no end. Imagine your arms and legs flailing about, quivering and twitching, and being helpless to stop them or regulate their activity. This lack of neuromuscular maturity is one of the biggest reasons babies cry when left alone on their backs. How do you turn this agitated baby into a happy baby? Pick her up and hold her close to your body. Like puzzle pieces, your body and hers fit together in a way that minimizes those annoying disorganized movements.

Holding your infant close to your body lets her feel pressure from all directions, as she felt in the womb. It keeps her in the fetal tuck, the most calming and comfortable position for infants and the one that helps their digestion and temperature regulation.

Holding baby steadily for much of the day (a baby sling helps tremendously) greatly reduces the number of times she is vulnerable to the Moro, or startling, reflex. Picking a baby up and putting her down frequently is not as beneficial, since she's likely to startle each time you release her.

19.

To swaddle or not to swaddle?
Let baby decide.

Some newborns crave the contained feeling they get from being tightly wrapped in a soft blanket. It helps them keep their limbs from flailing and also from the Moro reflex. For many, a nice tight swaddle is like an extra layer of hug. The feeling of pressure all around baby's body reminds him of the feeling of being in the womb—the more the pressure surrounds him, the more intense the association and therefore the comfort.

When baby lies unwrapped in a crib or bassinet, however, the pressure comes only from underneath him, which is not nearly as familiar or comforting. Most babies when left in cribs will seek out additional pressure by pushing whatever part of their bodies they can into the bumpers or wedging themselves up into a corner. What they are really looking for, of course, is your warm body to snuggle up against, but in its absence, they will settle for anything that adds to their sense of being surrounded.

Yet for some babies, the confinement of swaddling is an unwelcome restraint. These babies just hate it. Try loose, comfortable clothing as well as swaddling and see which your baby likes best. Trial and error is the only route to getting to know your baby, so pay attention to his responses to everything you do.

20.

Share baths and massages with baby.

For the first few months it's likely that baby will not like being bathed. She doesn't need a bath every day. Once or twice a week is fine. But the best way to have a happy infant at bath time is simply to bring her into the tub with you. Baby is likely to love the feel of the warm water if she can enjoy the comfort of your arms or Daddy's hairy chest.

Adjust the temperature of the bathwater to baby's tastes—lukewarm or cool water is more appropriate for baby's thinner, more sensitive skin than the hot water you're probably used to. You can buy bathtub floater toys that indicate 91 to 97 degrees Fahrenheit, the comfort range for a baby's bathwater. You might want to lower your water heater thermostat to 120 degrees to eliminate any chance of scalding.

Older babies usually enjoy baths, even solo, especially if they include tub toys, songs, and lots of loving attention from you. Soapy massages feel great on hardworking little muscles, and the tub is an ideal setting for name-the-body-part games.

Many object to the shampoo-rinsing step, though. Tuck hated having to tilt his head backward. But he didn't mind if I poured water on top of his head from a cup and let it run down all over him. Be sure to use no-tear shampoo!

After her bath, treat baby to a massage. Sharon Heller, Ph.D., in her fascinating book, *The Vital Touch,* says that babies who are massaged are "more social, more alert, less fussy and restless, sleep better, and have smoother movements. They enjoy playing with their mothers, who, in turn, enjoy their babies more."

Massage makes baby healthier too! According to Dr. Heller, it can improve the functioning of the immune system throughout life. In addition, "Massage stimulates circulation of the blood and lymph fluids, fuels the muscles with fresh oxygen and nutrients while flushing away metabolic waste products, releases physical tension, and soothes the nerves by lowering the stress hormones cortisol and norepinephrine and by releasing endorphins in the brain."

Check your library or bookstore for a book that teaches the best ways to give infant massages. Two good ones are *Baby Massage* by Amelia D. Auckett and *Infant Massage: A Handbook for Loving Parents* by Vimala Schneider.

21.

See the world through baby's eyes.

Babies live completely and utterly in the present moment. They have no concept of a past or future. The situation that baby is presently in feels like all eternity to him. If he's uncomfortable, there is no consolation in the imagined possibility that things will get better.

The first few months of a baby's life are probably like living in a waking dream. Objects appear and disappear; noises come and go out of nowhere. Smells, colors, and lights are observed without any understanding of their origin. Babies just take it all in and gradually learn to make sense of it.

Until they do, YOU are baby's world. Your baby will recognize and take comfort in your voice and smell within a few hours of his life. Within a few weeks, he will recognize your face. Most experts believe that babies don't realize they are separate beings. When mommy sings, baby is likely to have the sensation "We're singing."

Memory starts to kick in typically at around three or four months. That's when baby starts to remember other people and things he has regular contact with. He'll like his special and familiar people best and will take great comfort in those parts of his day that remain constant, like nursing and spending time in his baby sling. You will still be the most important thing in his life, but he will at least begin to acknowledge that there are other interesting things aside from mommy.

22.

Spend your baby bucks on things that will make baby happy.

Everyone sets aside a certain amount of money to spend on a new baby. How much you have available to spend is not nearly as important as how you spend it. Babies don't need their own rooms. Parents enjoy decorating and furnishing a baby's room far more than the baby enjoys spending time in it. In fact, if the plan is to leave baby alone in her room for bedtime or any other time, then this expenditure is likely to contribute more to her unhappiness than to her happiness. If you really want to decorate a nursery and you have plenty of money to spend, by all means do so, but try to think of it as a storage place for baby's clothes and toys—not as a place where baby is to live.

Happy babies don't need cribs, strollers, swings, play yards, or high chairs. All of these contraptions just serve to separate babies from contact with humans, which makes babies miserable. The following few Ways will give you ideas for how to spend that bundle of bucks I just saved you. And if you're still pregnant and haven't had a baby shower yet, read on for revisions to your wish list!

23.

Instead of buying a crib, take your baby into your bed.

All over the world, parents take their babies to bed with them, and not just in cultures that differ greatly from our own. Every morning, babies in Japan, Africa, Israel, Mexico, and Sweden wake up contented and secure in the company of their loved ones. And while many American baby care advisors are still handing out yesterday's advice about babies sleeping alone, surveys have found that 25 to 30 percent of Americans aren't listening to them.

In addition to all of the health and bonding reasons listed elsewhere in this book, they do it because it feels so darn good. Sure, it takes some adjustment, but once you get used to that snuggly little warm body next to you at night, you can't help but recognize how right it is. Especially if you've had a hectic day or if you've had to be away from baby more than you'd like, nighttime is a calm, protected haven for catch-up loving. If the bed you're in now is too small for an extra occupant, why not spend some of that money you would have spent decorating the nursery on a bigger bed for you, your husband, and baby?

Another option is to buy a co-sleeper. They're sold in baby catalogs and in many of the larger chain stores that sell baby furniture. A co-sleeper is like a bassinet that attaches to the side of your bed so that baby can sleep next to you. They don't offer as much opportunity to cuddle, but co-sleepers can be just the thing for those parents who are initially nervous about having a tiny baby share their bed.

A popular option is the Arm's Reach co-sleeper, which later converts to a play yard. (I don't recommend ever putting your baby in a play yard, but they make fine toy boxes!)

If you've already got a standard-issue crib, you can easily use it to extend your bed space. Just remove one of the crib's side railings, and then position that side right next to your bed, getting it as close as possible. Also, adjust the crib mattress so that it is at the same level as your bed's mattress. If the mattresses don't meet evenly enough for your peace of mind, you can buy a foam rubber device called a bed bridge and cut it to fit your needs. Bed bridges are made to fill in the space between two adjacent twin beds, turning them into a king-size bed, so they're sold wherever you buy your bedding, not in baby stores.

I actually like the transformed crib arrangement more than the co-sleeper because it gives all of the bed occupants more space. We've set up Tuck's crib this way, and most mornings we find some portion of mine or my husband's body borrowing the crib space, with Tuck in the middle of the bed.

There is no way to describe the deliciousness of waking up with a happy, affectionate baby. I would be hard-pressed to say which of the three of us benefits the most from that half hour of laughing, tickling, and snuggling that starts each of our days, but I know we'd be a different family without it.

24.

Instead of buying an expensive stroller, buy several baby slings.

Wear baby in a sling when you go out. It only *sounds* exhausting; you really do get used to it! You'll get so accustomed to wearing him that you'll feel strange without him. Remember that babies are like little weight-trainers, gradually increasing your muscle strength so that it's easier and easier for you to carry them.

Babies confined in strollers for every excursion miss out on invaluable learning! If they are lying down, all they see is the sky or the inside of the stroller. If they are sitting up, all they see is a scary, distorted, knee-high view of the world. All they hear is random noise and all they feel is the rigid stroller against their bodies.

Think about how much more your baby will benefit if he's up at chest level, right next to you. He smells your smells, hears your voice, feels your warmth and your touch. As you talk to him about the things you pass, he gets the opportunity to enjoy your presence, your laugh, your world. He feels valued as your companion. He is *connected*; he gets to view the mall, the park, your neighborhood—wherever you take him—the way you view it, the way he will when he becomes a full-grown member of society.

In addition to this mode of transportation being better for baby, it's better for you too! The moms I know who routinely use slings instead of strollers truly enjoy taking their babies with them wherever they go. They don't consider their babies an inconvenience at all—on the contrary, they think of the babies as welcome companions who make the outings more fun.

You may want to get an inexpensive umbrella stroller (around $20) for times when you'll need to carry other items as well as baby. When I go shopping, Tuck's always in the sling, but I often bring the umbrella stroller along to pile my purchases in! It's good for toting a heavy diaper bag too, though you rarely need to take your whole diaper bag out of the car because baby slings make great carryalls. I don't even bring a purse with me anywhere. I slip one diaper in the bottom of the sling, under Tuck's tush, along with a plastic resealable bag with a few wipes in it. My wallet (which also houses my keys) gets slipped behind Tuck's back. The sling serves as a changing pad.

Believe me, this routine is a lot easier than hauling a stroller out of the trunk, wrestling it open, filling it with a bulky diaper bag and a loudly protesting baby, maneuvering it through crowds, and searching for those ever elusive elevators in stores and public buildings! (See Way 15 for the best slings and how to purchase them.)

25.

Don't rely on baby containers.

The baby swing has become a dangerously popular baby-sitter. While it is true that your baby will prefer motion to lying static in some other type of container, the motion of the swing is not the kind he craves. Babies need the variety of movement that being carried by an active human provides. The monotonous back and forth of a swing can lull babies into trancelike states that do nothing for their development. The helpless little zombies will often retreat into an unhealthy sleep to shut out the repetitive stimulation. Better to use your budget to hire a reliable child from your neighborhood to hold your baby while you do whatever it was you had hoped to accomplish while she was swinging.

Playpens (their politically correct name is play yards) serve no other purpose than to hold toys and baby things. Take the time to baby-proof your house so that you don't have to put your mobile baby in a cage. Doing so severely limits her opportunities to grow and develop at her own pace.

High chairs aren't an unwise purchase if used only for brief mealtimes, but many babies eat much better and more willingly in a parent's lap. After about eighteen months, baby might graduate to a booster seat at the family table, which costs much less, takes up less space, and gives baby a greater sense of belonging.

Of course, there will be times throughout the day when baby cannot be in your arms (or anyone else's). It's fine to put her down on the carpet or on a soft, clean blanket where she can see you. Just keep these sessions as brief as possible if baby does not enjoy them. Once baby is sitting on her own she'll like being on the floor much more.

26.

Help baby cope with car seat anxiety.

There is one baby-containing piece of equipment that you'll have to buy and use: a car seat. Most car seats made especially for infants can be easily snapped out of the car and used as baby carriers. Since babies often fall asleep in moving cars, a snap-out carrier allows you to remove baby from the car without waking her. Don't rely on the carrier for much else, however. This type of container deprives baby of much-needed human contact and many important learning experiences. Slings are far better for transporting awake babies, but a lift out of the car seat into the sling wakes some sleeping babies, and for that reason alone, snap-out seats can be helpful.

 Newborn babies often like the lulling sensation of a ride in the car, but as they mature, most babies go through at least one period of NOT liking being strapped into a car seat. As their inner-ear mechanisms develop, some babies may be more prone to motion sickness. Plus, it can be hard for baby to understand why you won't hold her when she knows you're right there and can hear her request. The separation is especially hard on babies who must face backward in a backseat alone.

 If your baby is going through a difficult time with the car, try to travel when she's rested, full, and comfortable. Have a few new soft toys to offer. (New doesn't have to mean store-bought. It could mean a colorful sock with an old rubber squeak toy inside, tied at the top with some textured ribbons and yarn.) Sing happy songs and talk to baby so that she knows you're close by, and avoid long trips alone with her if you can. Build in extra travel time so that if baby is really upset, you can pull over, take her out of her seat, and nurse or comfort her a little before resuming your trip.

Whenever possible during this trying phase, have someone else drive so you can ride next to baby in the back. She's likely to be much happier with some company to sing and play with. Show her things out the window as you pass them. It's easy to nurse baby by just leaning over the car seat a little.

If you have to be alone with baby in the car and she's especially upset about the situation, try this trick my friend Abby uses with her baby, Jessica. If Jessica starts fussing while Abby's en route somewhere, Abby pulls into a parking lot and nurses her *in the car seat* until she falls asleep. Once Jessica is soundly sleeping, Abby can resume driving.

27.

Learn to stay cool when baby can't.

Your newborn baby may cry a lot. He'll cry to signal his needs, but he can't easily distinguish between feelings of hunger, cold, hot, wet, or loneliness. He just knows he feels bad and any bad feeling is a legitimate trigger for a bout of crying. He needs you to make it right.

Luckily for him, nature has designed you to be exceedingly uncomfortable when he is crying. Aside from your tender maternal concern for his welfare, your body goes haywire from the sound of his cries. Stress hormones are released into your bloodstream. Your blood pressure and breathing rate increase. Your muscles tense. The louder the cries and the longer they go on, the more mayhem is wreaked on your body's basic physiological systems. All this because nature wants to be sure that you DO SOMETHING to make your baby feel better. Your instinct to comfort him and his instinct to signal a need for comfort are in cahoots. Together, the two instincts ensure the survival of our species.

Even when their obvious needs are met and they are being held and walked, some babies just cry more than others. Sometimes nothing seems to help. A parent can feel guilty or angry or guilty for feeling angry, but any negative emotion just makes the situation worse. If you've thoroughly checked for every possible problem baby may be having and tried every possible remedy and baby is still crying, hold him close and try to stay calm yourself since that's the only way you'll be able to calm him.

Sympathy for baby's anguish is the best emotion for you to feel. If an adult friend had suffered a loss that made him inconsolable, your feelings would probably be lovingly supportive and you would want to do anything you could do to help while realizing that you are unable to fix the loss for your friend. Try to develop that mind-set with your baby.

Sometimes there's nothing a parent can do to ease baby's upset, but holding him and saying soothing words will let baby know that he doesn't have to suffer alone, that you care about his suffering, and that you will do all you can to help. Remember, the problem is not your fault, and not baby's either. Some babies just have a more difficult time getting accustomed to a very strange new world.

In those first few weeks, baby could even still be affected by drugs used during delivery. If you experienced a high level of stress in delivery, your stress hormones could be remaining in baby's system, and his cries could be a release of the tension they're causing him.

28.

Ignore anyone who tells you your baby is manipulating you!

One of the most significant barriers to raising happy babies is the bizarre notion that our babies are trying to control us. I don't know what paranoid parent first thought up this absurdity, but unfortunately it has caught on to the extent that many parents view their tiny babies suspiciously from the start!

Look at your baby's face. Does she really look like she's plotting strategies to manipulate you into doing her bidding? Is that innocent look of helpless devotion a clever ruse? Of course not! She's a baby! Get over yourself and realize that this tiny creature is completely dependent on you for every aspect of her survival. If she seems a little demanding, cut her some slack. She's programmed to need you, not because of some perverse pleasure she takes in ruining your life, but simply because human babies cannot survive without lots of help from attentive adults. Taking care of her is what you signed on for when you made the decision to bring her into this world.

You may be thinking of some particular toddler you know who very much fits the description of a manipulator. Babies are extremely sensitive to their parents' feelings and expectations, and the sad consequence of the babies-as-manipulators mentality is that many parents have caused their children to become exactly what they feared. If parents repeatedly act defensively with them and treat the children as if they are the enemy, the children will almost certainly fulfill their parents' expectations.

If, on the other hand, parents lovingly recognize that toddlers are naturally strong-willed and often temperamental, not to mention loud and insistent in voicing their desires, these parents can use toddler-taming strategies that don't aggravate the habits they are meant to curb.

First and foremost, when disciplining your child, don't take anything she does personally. When angry or upset, lots of toddlers bite or hit their parents. This doesn't mean they are wild or bad or mean-spirited; it just means they are toddlers. By all means say a firm "no" and redirect the behavior, but don't feel betrayed and angry over what is a natural and age-appropriate expression of emotion.

Believe in the psychic bond you can develop with your baby.

Many well-meaning parents doubt their own abilities when it comes to listening to their preverbal babies. They wonder how they can possibly develop a reliable communication system. The answer lies in spending time with your baby!

Think about your loving relationship with your spouse, or best friend, or maybe a sibling. Often in our close relationships with other adults, the slightest change in facial expression lets us know exactly what our loved one is thinking. Such bonds develop through shared experiences. The more time you spend in direct contact with any person, the more enmeshed you become, and the more intuitive you are about that person's feelings. It works the same way with baby. And sleep time counts too! Being near your baby during the night enhances your connection during the day.

For a bond to grow, communication must grow, so be responsive to baby's signals. The more you make a point of trying to read baby, the more his efforts at communication will be rewarded, and the more effort he'll put into his communication attempts.

Baby-wearing Inuit and !Kung mothers are so in sync with their precious cargo that they know when their babies are about to urinate or have bowel movements! These amazing women feel the little gurgle in the baby's belly or the tensing of the limbs just in time to hold baby out away from their bodies—long enough for baby to complete his natural function. Then they tuck baby back in beside them, skin-to-skin, and carry on with their work!

I've heard at least one anecdote of such psychic communication working in the other direction. My attachment-parenting friend swears by an unorthodox remedy for her baby Chloe's constipation. She wears Chloe in the sling against her body while she, the mommy, successfully defecates in the usual manner. Immediately following this display, Chloe is able to complete her business, as if her mother's digestive system had mystically transferred instructions to Chloe's less experienced one. Weird!

30.

Don't make baby a shut-in.

If your baby gets a clean bill of health after the first few weeks, there's no reason to keep her confined in your home. Babies love being outside. You can often soothe a crying baby by just walking out your front door. And while car seats aren't always a hit, being in an interesting new environment often is.

Lots of moms think they're doing right by their babies by keeping them in the safely contained environments of their homes. But moms can go stir-crazy doing this, particularly if they were active before baby arrived. What's best for baby is having a mommy who's happy and enthusiastic, so treat yourself to some fun!

Young babies don't have any interests yet, so feel free to indulge your own. Take baby in the sling to an art museum, if that's what you like, or to an outdoor concert, or to your favorite store or restaurant. If you've worked most of your adult life and through your pregnancy too, make the most out of this home-with-baby time!

You'll want to keep baby's needs your top priority, but chances are that being held against your body as you participate in an activity you enjoy will be just what the baby ordered. Put simply, mommies who laugh and smile a lot usually have babies who do the same. Don't ever feel selfish during your baby's infancy for doing things that make YOU happy. As long as you include baby in your activities, the pursuit of your own happiness and that of baby's are practically one and the same. How will baby ever learn the fine art of joyfulness without a consistent and convincing model?

When baby announces he's hungry, pull the sling up for privacy and nurse him as you walk. (Or stop to bottlefeed him.) If he needs a diaper change, lay the sling down on any relatively soft surface for an instant changing pad. If he's tired, a slung, cuddled baby will fall asleep happily against your chest.

I even know one attachment-parenting mom whose baby was so predictably mellow that she was able to take personal growth classes with baby content in the sling the whole time. (She sometimes walked back and forth across the back of the classroom when her baby indicated he'd prefer some movement.)

Take Dad along too! Unless it's nursing time, let your husband wear baby in the sling. Dads have a different feel, a different gait, and often a higher perch from which baby can look out on the world. Tucker prefers facing out when his dad wears him in the sling, though with me, he prefers to straddle my hip. It's good for baby to get used to enjoying each of his primary caretakers' different styles of being with him.

My husband and I have never missed a party, a wedding, or a night out with friends in the year and a half since Tucker was born, and we've never once done any of those things without him. As a result, he's used to our social scene and he almost always happily cooperates. He's especially amazing at movie theaters. As long as we time it so that he's likely to be sleepy, he reliably nods off during the coming attractions as I sway in the back of the theater with him nursing in the sling. Once he's asleep, I sit down and comfortably enjoy the movie with him slumbering peacefully on my chest. (I always avoid loud and violent movies because I don't want him to subconsciously absorb any yucky stuff.)

As with any outing you take your baby on, be mentally prepared to leave or step outside if baby needs a break from whatever it is you're doing. Try to maintain an attitude of "I'll do this as long as he's happy and I'll stop when he's not." Then if you do have to stop or leave, just be grateful for the time you were able to spend before his needs called you away. Having to leave a function beats sitting at home and not even trying to attend it.

31.

Don't turn into a mommy-zombie.

Sleep deprivation is probably one of the biggest causes for postpartum depression. It can make the whole experience of new motherhood feel powerfully overwhelming and rob you of many of the joys of caring for your baby. The mommy-zombie condition is the result of being out of sync with baby and therefore waking much more than necessary throughout the night.

Baby isn't the only one who suffers when he sleeps alone. As a new mother, you are as biologically programmed to sleep next to baby as he is to sleep next to you. You may think that you'll get more sleep by sleeping apart from baby, but the reverse is probably true.

Your hearing is especially sharp after you give birth, and babies can be noisy sleepers. But if you have your room monitor adjusted properly, baby's noises will be louder over the monitor than if baby were next to you. They will also be more grating because of the electrical interference. Plus they're harder to interpret correctly because you can't feel or see baby to help in assessing his condition.

Your natural protective instincts are heightened when separated physically from your baby, so you're much more apt to interpret noises as threats to baby's welfare than if he were right beside you. So you hear a little whimper, and you jump out of your warm bed and rush down the hall to baby's room. Maybe he's sleeping fine, but it may take you half an hour to get back to sleep. If he had been beside you, you might not have woken at all.

Or maybe baby has woken up and he needs help getting back to sleep. By the time you reach him, he's likely to be fully aroused and crying in earnest. It will take much longer to get him back to sleep than if he had been beside you and you had only to cuddle or nurse him at the first sign of his waking.

It turns out that Mother Nature has taken care of the whole sleeping problem for us, if we would only provide the right conditions for her perfect solution. When mothers and babies sleep together, and especially when baby is breastfed, their sleep cycles align themselves to a mutual internal clock! Amazing as it sounds, research has proved that the close nighttime contact shared by co-sleeping mothers and babies causes them to go through periods of light and deep sleep at the same times throughout the night.

Practically speaking, that means baby doesn't ever wake Mommy from the deep sleep she so badly needs. When baby goes through a light-sleep stage (the stage during which babies wake) Mommy is going through one too, so she'll often wake up about thirty seconds before baby does, anticipating his need for mothering. When baby starts to stir, Mommy can just pull him in close to her and nurse him back to sleep before he ever fully arouses. Mommy, barely having moved, can easily drift back to sleep too.

I found this phenomenon hard to believe when I first read about it, but it has been working for me for over a year now, and many of my friends enjoy it too. Don't expect it to take effect the first night, though. You may have to sleep with baby for a few weeks before the two of you are completely in sync. And if you didn't sleep with baby from birth, taking him into your bed may not go smoothly for the first few weeks. It takes time for the bed partners to adjust to one another's company, but the rewards more than compensate for any loss of sleep during the brief transition period.

If you're unlucky enough to have one of those people in your life who says things like "Aren't you afraid you'll roll over on him and suffocate him?" thank her for her concern but let her know she's misinformed. While freak accidents like that do happen, they are extremely rare—about as common as babies dying accidental deaths alone in their cribs—and almost always due to the parent being under the influence of drugs or alcohol.

You have an awareness called your proprioceptive sense that keeps you from rolling onto your baby. It's the same sense that keeps you from rolling out of bed and from rolling onto your spouse or pet as you sleep. Position baby away from soft pillows, don't allow baby to sleep on a waterbed, and make sure everyone sharing the bed is 100 percent sober. Then put the rolling-over worry out of your mind and start getting the sleep you need to enjoy your happy baby.

32.

Think like a mama kangaroo!

With only 25 percent of their adult brain size, human babies are born more immature than any other animals. Unlike baby dogs, cats, horses, and elephants, who can all walk within a short time of being born, baby humans are simply incapable of autonomous functioning. Even apes, our closest mammalian relatives, are born with 45 percent of their brains developed, a level most human babies don't reach until close to the end of their first year, when they are crawling.

The problem is that human brains grow so fast that babies' heads would never make it through the vaginal canal if the babies didn't exit at around nine months. That's why our babies are born so totally dependent on us. Looking to nature for the best way to handle this early delivery situation (in a way, human babies are all extreme preemies!), we should take our cues from marsupials, since they are the only mammals born more dependent on their mothers than humans are. Mama kangaroo's solution, of course, is to keep her baby right against her body in her pouch until he matures enough to venture out on his own. Just as kangaroos' bodies are outfitted with the right equipment for baby holding, humans' hips and arms are designed for easy baby-carrying. A baby sling makes it even easier.

Almost all mammal mothers spend more time in close contact with their babies than humans typically do, in spite of the animals' greater maturity level at birth. Infant monkeys are almost never apart from their mothers during the first year of life.

If they are forcibly separated, their little systems freak out. Stress hormones flood their bodies, their heart beat rates increase, and their immune systems go haywire. Returning to their mothers brings their bodies mostly back to normal, but their sleep patterns and immune systems can suffer long-term effects. Primates are our closest relatives in nature, and many experts believe that separation of human babies from their mothers is close on the trauma scale to that of infant monkeys.

Once again, this biological evidence supports the theory that an appropriate human gestation period is at least eighteen months: nine months in and nine months out of the womb. During that second nine months, babies should have almost continuous contact with their mothers; their needs should be met immediately, as when they were in the womb.

It may sound like a difficult way to raise a baby, but once you start practicing this attached style of parenting, you will be amazed at how easy it is and how much it can simplify your life. It practically eliminates frustration for babies, and that means far fewer frustrations for parents as well!

33.

Involve baby in your life.

The most famous baby-care guru of the past few generations warned that if you held your baby too much she would forget how to amuse herself, feel bored, deserted, and miserable when left alone, and cry for attention. For many years, moms trusted this expert more than they trusted themselves, so they suffered through the anguish of letting their babies lie helpless and alone. Today it is thankfully acknowledged that babies are *supposed* to feel bored, deserted, and miserable when left alone, and they will certainly cry for attention, no matter how much they have been held. A baby who stops crying for attention when left alone has probably just given up hope.

Babies are not meant to "amuse themselves." They are not even meant to be by themselves. And when they are close to their caregivers, they don't need amusement at all. When they feel right, because of their proximity to loving adults, they are perfectly content to watch and learn about their world. Babies don't need lots of play or even attention to keep them from being bored. A baby gets all the stimulation he needs simply by being held by an active adult as she goes about her daily work. If the adult talks to baby about what she is doing, all the better!

Babies like action. They love being involved in your cooking, cleaning, shopping, walking, and laundry folding. Babies naturally build up tension in their bodies, which is released through motion. Since they can't yet provide much motion for themselves, they need you to do it for them.

Babies who are forced to lie still for long periods in a bassinet, baby carrier, or stroller will become frustrated because they have no outlet for the inevitable buildup of tension. All they want is to feel included in the active lives of their caregivers.

34.

Exercise with baby!

After waddling around in slow motion for the last few months of your pregnancy, you probably feel gratefully light on your feet, even if your body isn't quite what it was ten months before. Celebrate by exercising! But don't make the mistake of dumping baby off at Grandma's so you can solo it to the gym. Most babies love to indulge the habits of an active mama. If the weather is welcoming, plop baby in the sling and go for power walks around the neighborhood. The even distribution of baby's weight, thanks to the sling, will enhance your aerobic workout.

Talk to him about all the things you see as you pass them. It's my observation that babies are more receptive to learning things when they're outdoors. If you walk often enough with your preverbal baby, you will be astonished at how quickly he later learns the words for all those familiar sights. By fourteen months, Tuck knew *tree, grass, dog, sidewalk, bird, stop sign, mailbox, doorbell, car,* and *vroom!* all from his regular walks in the sling.

In bad weather, try this fun alternative with your premobile baby: Prop up baby in a spot where he can see you. Play some fast, upbeat music, and dance wildly in front of him. He'll think you are fascinating and you'll be getting a great workout. If it's dark, you could even arrange the lighting in the room so that your dancing creates a shadow show on the wall behind you. Once baby becomes a toddler, he'll love to dance along.

When baby gets old enough to support his head easily, you can do the following exercises while holding him. (Tucker loved our exercise program, and he clearly thought the whole routine was done solely for his amusement.)

♡ baby crunches. Lie on your back and pull up your knees to your chest. Then place baby on your shins, so he's lying on his stomach with his face peering over your knees and the two of you are facing each other. While holding baby in place with your hands, straighten your legs out and then bring them back in. Make a funny noise or face or both every time you bring baby toward you and your exercising efforts will be rewarded with delicious baby giggles—the ultimate incentive to keep at it!

♡ the baby march. This is great for thigh and butt muscles. Hold baby against your body with baby facing out. Then walk around the house, taking giant steps and bending down low with each step so that you feel the big muscles in your legs and butt working. Try singing a slow, funny song in a low voice while doing this for extra silliness. Baby gets an interesting up-and-down tour of the house, and you get a real body-sculpting session!

♡ sit-ups. Believe it or not, these are more fun with baby on your stomach, leaning back against your thighs. Just make sure baby is old enough not to fall off sideways. As you lower your head, fingers laced behind your head, bring your elbows together over your face and say, "Where's Mama?" Then, as you raise your head, open your elbows and say, "Peekaboo!" or "Here's Mama!" or whatever makes baby smile most.

♡ push-ups. Just lie baby on his back on the floor, and do push-ups over him, bringing your face down close to his with each repetition.

♡ leg lifts. Lie on your side with baby next to you on the floor, and sing or recite nursery rhymes in sync with your movements.

35.

Let your baby's independence develop naturally.

There is absolutely no need to train a child to become independent. If allowed to grow and blossom in their own ways, at their own rates, children will naturally become independent. When we force them into independence before they are ready, all we are doing is hopelessly undermining their confidence in themselves and in the world, thereby ironically, making them much more needy and dependent. Yet in our country, many experts advise early independence "training" that causes much unhappiness for babies.

Training is not for human infants. We train dogs because in order to live with them, we need them to become very different animals than if left to their own natures. We train our pets not according to what's best for the animals, but according to what's most convenient and pleasant for us, the owners. Human infants are meant to be dependent, and to try to train them to be otherwise is to deny a real aspect of their humanness.

Children know how much nurturing they need at any given time. They will not ask for more than is necessary for their optimal growth. Overnurturing happens only when a parent continually rushes to comfort even though the child has not indicated any need for comforting. If a parent listens carefully as the child signals her needs for nurturing, the child will always get the correct "dose."

It's the babies who cry out for attention and are not given it who will have a lingering sense of longing and never be satisfied. Babies who are always given the love they ask for will have no anxieties about being abandoned or losing their vital connection with loved ones. They are the ones who will develop that deep sense of security and well-being that allows for true independence and happiness. A child whose needs are met and who has a strong attachment to her parents establishes a foundation of trust that will allow her to become independent.

Understanding and meeting a baby's needs not only makes her feel loved but teaches her how to love too. Child development specialist Selma Fraiberg explains the feeling of love and intimacy between a mother and child as the child's first falling-in-love experience. If this first love is free of frustration, anger, disappointment, and fear of abandonment, a child stands a much better chance of finding secure, healthy love as an adult.

Most adults in America today were raised during the years when early independence training was strongly urged by then popular experts. And we're a mess! Never before have so many Americans regularly attended support groups and paid therapists to help them overcome their dependencies.

Self-help books sell in record quantities. Apparently, independence training hasn't worked!

36.

Let baby touch it!

Your baby doesn't just *want* to touch everything in sight—he *needs* to! Touching is one of the most important ways babies learn. Here's a trick that might save you some frustration: Before your baby hits the crawling stage, make a point of letting him touch everything that attracts his attention. Sometimes he'll want to touch things that could be dangerous if he were to later come across them unsupervised, but it's still best not to keep these things off-limits entirely. That will only heighten their mysterious appeal and make the most dangerous things in your house the most enticing ones for baby.

With baby in your arms, take him on a tour of your home's baby-proofed electrical outlets, stopping at each one long enough for him to touch and thoroughly examine it. Let him push the buttons on the stove, the dishwasher, and the telephone. Hold a closed pair of scissors by the dangerous end while he examines the safe end and sucks on the handles.

If you do this often enough before he learns to crawl, your baby will have no need to head straight for every danger zone as soon as he's mobile enough to do so. Babies are notorious for doing that simply because the things that have been kept from them are the very things they've become most curious about. If your baby's already grown bored with the taboo stuff, it will be easier for you to direct his attention to appropriate playthings once he's getting around on his own.

When he's old enough to understand rules better, you can verbally direct his touching and help him to recognize what's off-limits. Dr. William Sears recommends saying "yes touch" for safe things, "no touch" for unsafe things, and "soft touch" for people and animals. To curb grabbing, he suggests "one-finger touch."

37.

Help baby become aware of her own body.

Baby becomes aware of her body by how it relates to your body. To understand where she begins and ends, she touches you and realizes that her fingers in her mouth feel different from her fingers in your mouth. The more you make regular contact with your baby, the sooner she will make this distinction.

Since a psychological sense of self grows out of a physical sense of self, a strong awareness of her body is one of baby's first steps toward healthy self-esteem. The more complete the body contact and the more time spent in contact with you, the stronger the association for baby. In *The Vital Touch,* Sharon Heller, Ph.D, speculates that American babies, who are typically held on average for less than 25 percent of their day, are especially at risk for a number of psychological problems.

Since babies are designed for continual contact, the minimal contact that most American babies receive contributes to the widespread lack of respect American adults have for their bodies. Negative body image and disorders like anorexia nervosa and bulimia are epidemic in our society. Dr. Heller writes of our relationship with our bodies; "Stuffing them, starving them, imbibing them, implanting them, and tucking them, we neglect them, abuse them, and transform them. The one thing many seem unable to do is to love them."

Simplistic as it sounds, psychologists agree that the more love we felt from our parents, the more we are able to love ourselves. Similarly, the more physical love our little bodies received, the more we are able when the time comes to love our own big bodies.

38.

Celebrate your marriage while you celebrate your baby.

Happy marriages are necessary for happy babies. Babies pick up on every nuance of their parents' emotions, and a conflict-ridden marriage is an often overlooked cause of extra stress in babies. You and your husband need to recognize that together you have done a tremendous thing by creating this little person and also that turbulent emotions are common during any time of great transition. Keep the lines of communication open, and try to maintain a shared sense of humor about the very normal deprivations that come with new parenthood.

Many people are afraid that sharing their beds with their babies will hurt their marriages, particularly their sex lives. If a couple believes that, it could very well become a self-fulfilling prophecy. But there is no reason it needs to be that way. A great number of happy couples who sleep with their babies report that they never felt closer or more in love than when they were lying in bed together, gazing upon their perfect, tiny creation.

A shared love for a baby often awakens a new and exciting facet of marital love. Sleeping with your baby will bond you to her in the same way that sleeping beside your spouse helped bond the two of you. And it works for fathers too! Often fathers are unsure of the best ways to become important in their babies' lives. Co-sleeping is a wonderful way.

Of course, the bigger question for some people is "What about sex?" And many would answer that sex can be just as good, or even better when there is a baby in the bed. Babies will not be harmed in any way by witnessing a loving act between their parents. But even if you are uncomfortable with the baby in the same room, you have every other room in the house to experiment with—which can be a lot more fun than your previous routine!

The fact is that new parents typically do not have as much sex as they did when they were childless, and this has nothing at all to do with where in the house the baby sleeps. Some researchers maintain that a woman's low level of estrogen following childbirth reduces her sex drive, but that doesn't explain why so many new fathers also temporarily lose interest in sex. Maybe it's fatigue; maybe it's overwhelming infatuation with the new family member. It doesn't really matter what causes it.

I want to stress that there is absolutely nothing wrong with your marriage if you mutually agree to shelve lovemaking for a while. It's sad that our culture makes such a big deal out of sex that couples often start to doubt their marriages simply because they are surprised by how little sex they are having after a new baby enters the picture.

Societal mores tend to pendulum back and forth. A few generations ago, people felt something was wrong with them if they wanted too *much* sex. Today we think there's something wrong if we want too *little*. Whatever works for you and your husband is the perfect amount of sex, no matter how horrifying it may sound to your childless friends.

And neither is there anything wrong with you if you do experience a high level of interest in sex after your baby is born. Of course, if your interest level and your husband's go in opposite directions, that will feel like a problem! Just try to keep it in perspective. If the conflict is truly attributable to the baby, bear with one another and realize that your child's infancy is a very finite period in a long, loving marriage. The two of you will have many more years without an infant than you'll have with one. Besides, sexual feelings come and go in strong marriages for lots of reasons that have nothing to do with babies. This natural fluctuation in sex drive is nothing to worry about—it's the worrying that tends to cause problems.

39.

Handle your anger like a grown-up.

It is natural to get angry. Babies are exceptionally good at doing things that produce anger in parents. It is normal and expected that your baby's actions will sometimes make you want to scream. If you do scream, however, you are not behaving responsibly as a parent. An out-of-control caregiver is terrifying for a child. And your baby will not learn to improve her behavior by witnessing bad behavior on your part.

Chances are, at some point your baby will do all of these things: She won't sleep when you want her to. She will cry for what appears to be no good reason, sometimes for a very long time. She will vociferously object to being put down or being put in her car seat or being put in a bath. She will not eat when you think she should. She will eat much more messily than you would like. She will break things. She will prevent you from doing things you loved doing in your pre-baby life.

But if you feel anger rising up inside you whenever one of these perfectly natural events takes place, you could be sending your baby a dangerous message. Babies are unbelievably sensitive to the emotions of their parents. Even if you think you are hiding your anger, your baby is probably sensing it and applying it to herself. In the worst-case scenario, you could find yourself unable to keep your anger in check and lash out physically or verbally at your baby.

If you *occasionally* notice yourself feeling angry with your baby and make a real effort to act appropriately, you will not do your baby any serious harm. But if you are often angry, seek help. Get counseling, take up yoga, meditate, hire a mother's helper—but DO SOMETHING to break the pattern. Learning to get a grip on your anger could be the most worthwhile action you ever take on your child's behalf.

40.

Respect the rate at which baby's abilities develop.

Most babies follow a similar pattern of mastering physical and mental skills, though some may vary from the norm. Parents love to compare the rates at which their kids learn new tricks, despite the fact that it means absolutely nothing to be early or late. When they walk through the kindergarten classroom door, the child who sat up alone at four months will be no better at sitting than the child who didn't sit alone until she reached nine months.

A baby's personality and interests affect which skills he chooses to develop at any given time. A baby who is fascinated by practicing his fine-motor control may build block towers before he learns to walk, while another baby would never waste time sitting there with blocks when there's so much ground to cover and exploring to do. Some experts believe that the rate at which babies reach physical milestones is hereditary. So don't rush, and don't compare!

As a general rule, babies hone their skills from the top down and from the middle out. That means they first master head and eye control, then arm control, and finally leg control. And they make movements with their shoulders before they gain control of their hands and finally their fingers.

Babies are born with an innate drive to master more and more complex tasks. The best thing you can do to help is watch and encourage. Pay attention to your baby's preferences and try to provide him with the environments and props he seems to need to progress.

There is no need to actually teach your baby to sit, crawl, walk, or use his hands more effectively since these things will all happen for your baby when he is ready. (If baby is very far behind the norm, or if your instincts tell you there may be a problem, ask your doctor for a thorough assessment.)

When you see baby focusing on a new skill, don't distract him or try to help him. Encouragement and praise are great when they match baby's own obvious satisfaction at mastering something, but they can be detrimental when they interrupt or interfere with baby's efforts. Even at this very young age, babies can sense pressure from you. When baby accomplishes a new feat, he's likely to be excited about it, and that is the best time for you to share in baby's pride and happiness.

41.

Beware the "good baby" trap!

We all know one, either down the block or at the playgroup or in our family: the mommy who endlessly reminds you what a "good baby" she has. Her baby sleeps through the night. He eats, drinks, naps, and poops at exactly the same hour every day. He never cries. This mommy's not-so-subtle message to you is that she has her baby under control, she has trained him to be a convenient and exemplary child, and you would do well to listen to all of her child-rearing advice.

Run! Run away from her as fast as you can! Babies who don't bother anybody and accept whatever regimen is imposed upon them are often babies who have given up any hope of having their requests honored and their needs met. They are at risk for becoming withdrawn children, internally angry adolescents, and depressed adults. When babies are chronically left to cry, they usually go one of two ways: They either become openly angry and miserable, or they learn at an early age to stifle their feelings because no one cares how they feel anyway.

42.

If you can't be there, find the best care for your baby.

If you absolutely must work while your child is still very young, finding the best possible care situation for your baby needs to be your No. 1 priority. If you don't have a mother or mother-in-law who conveniently lives close by—and who has a heart of gold and no other daytime obligations—you'll have to look into the next-best options.

Spend as much money as you can. (That's the only place in this book where I'll say that.) For the first few years you can get away with spending practically nothing on clothes, equipment, toys, and food for your baby, but when it comes to hiring someone to care for her, you'll need to be willing to break the bank. Of course, the best situation may not be the most costly; the point is that you must eliminate cost as a consideration.

Since you'll be spending so much, go through that exercise one more time where you work out all the math (commuting expenses, wardrobe expenses, taxes, etc.) to see if you absolutely, truly do have to go back to work right away. Was it a decision you made before your baby was born? Many dedicated-to-their-profession women plan pregnancies without giving the tiniest thought to taking a few years off to spend with their babies. But until that going-back-to-work day comes, you can't possibly know what it is going to feel like to leave your baby for so many hours at a time. Lots of moms who are doing it will tell you it feels really, really bad.

Some women cite financial reasons for returning to work, when the reasons have more to do with self-esteem and identity issues. It's horrible that our culture values child rearing so little that almost any career elevates a woman to a higher social standing than the career of pure mothering. If in your heart you want to be at home, then it doesn't matter what profession you were trained to do; no work is more important than raising your baby.

And if your reason for working truly is financial, you have to ask yourself how badly you need the income. Almost all of us could step down a notch or two on our scale of living without endangering ourselves or our children. The money will always be there to be made; this particular child's infancy is fleeting and precious.

But let's say your reason is that you love your work and know you will only be happy if you continue it, or you are returning to a full-time job after spending as much time as you possibly could spare at home being a mommy. Don't feel guilty! Every situation is unique, and lots of studies have shown babies of working-parent families to be no worse for the wear, as long as they've received loving, high-quality care. The most important thing to remember, particularly as your baby grows older, is to always be emotionally available and communicative with your child when you *are* present.

The best scenario for your baby is to have a substitute caregiver who will treat her as much like you would as possible. And you must be able to come to terms with this person being very special in your child's life. You want someone who has taken care of babies before, who is cheerful and warm, who shares your parenting beliefs, and who is looking for long-term employment. You don't want baby to become attached to someone who will disappear.

Give yourself plenty of time to investigate all the possibilities and stay open to different options. While babies are generally more comfortable in their own surroundings, some moms have found excellent care in the homes of women certified to take care of children. Day care has its obvious disadvantages, but there are some good situations out there. (The smaller the number of children per adult, the better.) Ask lots of questions and trust your instincts when you're talking to the potential caregiver. If you don't instantly like her and get a warm feeling from her, your baby probably won't either.

43.

Set your caregiver up for success.

Okay, you've made your decision. Now don't even think about leaving your baby for at least another week, and several weeks if he has already entered the stage of stranger or separation anxiety. During this transition period, spend every day in the company of your child and the caregiver, together. You will, of course, have to begin paying the caregiver and this may seem like a tragic waste of money with you right there, but remember—this is your one big expenditure toward your baby's happiness. Try to get to know the person (or day care staff) yourself. Be friendly and smile when you speak to her. Your baby will pick up your attitude, and this will be his first clue that she's trustworthy. If the caregiver doesn't want to spend time with you and baby together, she's not the right person.

If you have chosen someone who cares for other children as well, this is your opportunity to see her in action. If she is caring only for your child, let your baby determine the pace at which he interacts with her. He'll likely go through a period where he needs to go back and forth between the two of you before he's ready to handle a complete handoff.

Make sure before you begin working that your baby is happily attached to the new caregiver. You'll know by the ease with which he goes to her and the length of time he's happy with her once you've left the room. You'll be glad you've invested this time when you're back at work wondering what your baby is doing at that very second. You'll be able to conjure up a comforting image much more easily than if you had gone on your way the moment you hired his new friend.

If your child is a toddler when you first decide to leave him with a caregiver, how you say good-bye can make a big difference in her success with him. Even if your child makes scenes over good-byes, never sneak out when he is busy playing because he may lose trust in you. Try to keep it short and affectionate. When parents hesitate or draw out their good-byes, their toddlers sense their anxiety and have a harder time parting. Even if you feel sad, try to act cheerful and avoid saying things like "I'll miss you." Your emotions are exceptionally contagious in this kind of situation.

And even when you think he is ready to be on his own, if he has a particularly hard time saying good-bye that first day, you may want to arrange to hang around until it's easier for him. An article in *Parenting* described a day care situation in which "one little girl sobbed nonstop on her first day—and her second and third. She definitely needed a longer time than the others to adjust, so her mother sat quietly in the room reading the newspaper for the next ten days. Finally, when we both agreed that the daughter was ready to stay alone, her mother said good-bye. That time there were no tears."

Babies would almost always prefer their mommies, but if your child's caregiver is loving and he's getting plenty of the right kind of attention, toss the guilt out the window. Be prepared, though, to step back in at times. There may be days or whole weeks when your baby simply needs you. Whether he's sick, going through a rough emotional growth spurt, or just inexplicably angst-ridden, you will have to make a decision between letting your child suffer and letting your work suffer. Listen to your heart and make that dreaded phone call to the office.

44.

Full-time mommies, unite!

A full 62 percent of American women with children under age six work outside the home, yet statistics show that most women who plan (before giving birth) to return to work regret their choice when it's time to leave the baby. For some the choice is reversible, but for others it's not. Mothers who do put their careers on hold often remark how lucky they feel to be able to stay at home and raise their children.

Being a full-time mommy is no easy job, though, especially when you take it upon yourself, as most full-time mommies do, to be a full-time housekeeper, cook, and errand runner as well. If you expect baby to play alone while you get things done, baby is likely to protest and the tension will mount in both of you. Let baby be involved in your activities. Housework and chores may take twice as long, but you'll be simultaneously interacting with baby, so think of it as getting two things accomplished at once!

One of the more enjoyable activities you and baby can share is cultivating friendships with other mommies and babies. As much as you and your baby love one another and as healthy as it is for you to spend all your time together, you may start to go bonkers with no daytime adult companionship, and it's good for baby to see other people too, including little people. According to anthropologist Margaret Mead, "The worst thing is just having the mother boxed up with her baby twenty-four hours a day, which nobody ever meant to have happen in the whole history of the human race."

If your parenting practices are in sync with those described in this book, you'll find many like-minded mothers in La Leche League. And while you certainly don't have to share parenting styles with every friend you make, you'll find it is easier to compare notes and plan activities with your babies when you're on the same general parenting path. (Avoid parenting debates with other moms. It's a sensitive subject for most people, and everyone wants to believe they're doing their best by their children.)

Many public libraries and bookstores have storytimes for babies where you could keep an eye out for friendly-looking mommies with babies your child's age. MOMS Clubs (Moms Offering Moms Support) are free and vary greatly in their activities from chapter to chapter. For information, send $2 to MOMS, 25371 Rye Canyon Road, Valencia, CA 91355, or e-mail momsclub@aol.com. You could even start your own playgroup by taking out an ad in your community paper or posting notices in nearby parks, places of worship, or community centers. I met a wonderful bunch of like-minded moms by responding to an ad for an "attachment-parenting playgroup."

There are lots of baby classes you can participate in with your infant too. Organizations like Gymboree, Mommy & Me, My Gym, Amanda's Place, and Kindermusic all purport to be for baby's benefit but as far as I can tell their greatest value is as a meeting ground for moms with similar-aged babies. (Okay, after six months or so, the babies also seem to enjoy the programs!)

It can really enhance your enjoyment of your baby to have friends who have babies too. Besides having all that new-mommy stuff in common with you, the moms at these groups and classes are likely to have similar schedules to yours, while many of your pre-baby friends may be working.

Even if you're a shy person who never found it easy to start up relationships with strangers, take a chance with one of these organizations. Openers like "How old is he?" and "Wow! He has your eyes!" are a lot easier to deliver than those cheesy lines we used for meeting guys back in our single days! Most new mothers love to talk to anyone who shows any interest in their offspring, especially if you begin with the perfunctory "He's so cute."

Once you've lined up a few good mommy-buddies, visit one another's houses frequently. As you spend more and more time with these women, your baby will get to know them, and eventually you'll be able to baby-sit for one another. You could even set aside a day of the week where you take turns entertaining one another's babies. Just think how much you could get done if you had a mom and her baby at your house, playing with your baby while you paid bills, scrubbed bathrooms, wrapped gifts, or took care of whatever it is that's been piling up for you!

45.

Ban the S word!

Mistrust all persons who use the *S*-word with you in reference to your baby. Babies cannot be spoiled. Babies who are responded to immediately and are frequently held grow up with a far greater sense of trust in the world and confidence in themselves than those who aren't. After all the studies that have been done, most people should know this by now.

Ignoring a crying baby only makes him become more miserable and frantic and insecure. He may eventually stop crying on his own, but only after he has absorbed the information that he is not worth his parents' time and attention. He will likely become a clingy, whiny toddler and then a child who is often fussing and unhappy.

Fear of spoiling is a tragic bond-inhibitor! *Newsweek* magazine has stressed the importance of an attentive mother-child relationship as the foundation upon which all learning and feelings are built. This all-important bond helps form the brain's circuits for learning language, math, music, and emotional maturity. It is the very soil from which the child's whole personality will blossom and grow.

Renown infant researcher Stanley Greenspan calls it "the essential partnership," and Sigmund Freud described the mother-baby bond as "unique, without parallel, established unalterably for a whole lifetime as the first love object and as the prototype of all later love relationships for both sexes."

In their wonderful book, *What Every Child Needs,* Elisa Morgan and Carol Kuykendall quote pediatrician Frederic Burke, who says, "I firmly believe that early physical experience with parents' loving hands and arms is imprinted in the child's mind; and while apparently forgotten, it has a tremendous influence on the child's ego and the kind of adolescent he or she becomes."

My friend Holly points out, "When fruit spoils, it's because it's been left alone to rot, so why do people think kids can be spoiled by too much attention? You can only 'spoil' a thing by neglecting it."

46.

Don't obsess over baby's health!

It's natural to worry about your baby's health, but the more you can relax, the happier baby will be. You are biologically programmed to do everything within your power to ensure that your baby stays healthy, but there is only so much you can do without making life unnecessarily difficult for you and for baby. Within reason, try to keep baby's environment germ-free by insisting on frequent hand washing for all baby handlers. Watch baby carefully for illness-signaling cues, change diapers frequently to avoid rashes, and make sure baby is properly nourished. Then put all dire thoughts out of your mind so that you can enjoy parenting your healthy child!

A friend confided to me that she constantly conjures up horrific mental images of her baby being seriously injured in her absence. Lots of parents are haunted by such imaginings, so don't feel crazy if you are among them! Humans are hardwired with a strong need to ensure the safety of their offspring, so as strange and unsettling as these visions seem, they serve the purpose of keeping us alert to our mission.

The best thing you can do to avoid panic attacks is to keep baby close to you as often as possible, including during the night. Nothing freaks a parent out like the fear of Sudden Infant Death Syndrome (SIDS). It's been highly publicized that babies are at a reduced risk for SIDS if they are placed on their backs to sleep, but that is not the only precaution you can take against this terrible source of anxiety for new parents. There is much evidence to support theories that co-sleeping reduces the chances of SIDS as well as helping regulate babies' digestive systems and other bodily functions.

SIDS researcher Dr. James McKenna writes, "Co-family sleeping in humans, during at least the first year, is a universal, specieswide normative context for infant sleep, to which both parents and infants are biologically and psychosocially adapted." He goes on to say that the pattern of infants sleeping close to their mothers "has developed over at least four million years of evolution as a specific response to the biological and social needs of the human infant."

Dr. McKenna's studies have shown that proximity to a breathing parent during sleep helps regulate baby's own breathing patterns, thus lessening the threat of SIDS. Geography backs up this research. The highest incidents of SIDS are in urban societies where most babies sleep alone, as in the United States, United Kingdom, Canada, and New Zealand. In urban societies where babies sleep with their mothers, as in Hong Kong, Stockholm, Tokyo, and Jerusalem, SIDS statistics are far lower.

In addition, if you're sharing your bed with baby, you'll be able to detect fever much sooner, enabling you to get it under control before it gets too high. Plus, you'll forge a closer bond with baby, making it easier for you to read her cues so you can better distinguish between illness and general grouchiness. And what better way to stop obsessing over baby's welfare than to have her right there under your wing?

47.

Let baby decide when to start eating solid foods.

If you're breastfeeding, your baby is eating well. There is no *nutritional* reason to start feeding him solid foods until well beyond the half-year mark. For developmental reasons, however, you'll want to be on the lookout for signs that baby would like to give it a try. When you are eating, does he reach for your food or open his mouth when you open yours? Most babies are very clear in their request for solid foods, making hungry faces and attempting to grab everything you try to eat.

Pediatricians generally recommend rice cereal as baby's first food (preferably mixed with your breast milk), but I like Dr. William Sears's suggestion of a little glob of mashed banana on your fingertip. He points out that your finger is soft and warm and baby is already familiar with it. If baby spits that first bite back out at you, he's giving you an unequivocal message. Hear it, and give him time before you offer solids again.

If baby swallows enthusiastically and opens up for more, you've officially begun the solid-food stage! There are lots of books about what to feed your baby, so I'll let you research that elsewhere. But to keep the eating baby a happy baby, you'll have to learn to trust his signals. Never force a baby to eat because you think he should eat. It's perfectly appropriate for breast milk or formula to make up about 90 percent of baby's diet at nine months, and for breastfed babies, that percentage would still be fine beyond his first birthday. If baby turns his head away, clamps his mouth shut, or just looks disinterested, honor his request to end a feeding. By the time he really *needs* to eat solid foods, he'll *want* to eat them, though you may have to be creative in your marketing of them.

48.

Once baby's eating solids, make them yummy!

Commercial baby foods used to contain sugars and starches until mommies got peeved about it and started protesting. Now most contain nothing but water and the food they're impersonating. They're presumably much healthier now, but they taste incredibly bland and a lot of babies won't eat them. I can't help but wonder if that little bit of sugar was such a bad thing if

it helped fill babies' tummies with green beans, turkey, and squash. Some experts maintain that babies don't crave sweet or seasoned food and they're happy with the bland stuff, but my experience and that of many of my friends has been otherwise. Tuck soundly rejected even the purest, organically grown prepared foods but took to eating heartily when I mushed up tastier, more seasoned versions for him.

Even when baby has begun eating in earnest, don't expect any consistency in her preferences. The foods she hates today she may love next week. The amount she's happy eating may vary greatly from day to day as well. Watch for her cues. It's her appetite, her stomach, her decision. Period. Babies will not let themselves starve. Your only job is to offer nourishing choices.

At around six months, most babies love practicing their fine-motor skills by picking up finger foods. Some babies may need to eat iron-rich foods at this point, and I've found Cheerios to be the most heartily welcomed iron-fortified finger food. (They do contain some sugar, though, so if you're a real health food mama, don't sue me.)

Since Tuck insisted on feeding himself almost from the beginning, I used to smear onto Cheerios whatever pulverized food I had created for him and dot his tray with these tiny canapés. The gooey puree made the Cheerios sticky on top and even easier to pick up! When he got older, I'd spread stuff onto pieces of cheese, thinly sliced apple, or whole-wheat bread cut up into little cubes.

At one year, baby may play with her food more than eat it. Distressing as this period may be for the neat freaks among us, baby does actually learn from this experimentation. At some point, however, you will want to begin curbing the smushing, dropping, and throwing tendencies. You know your baby best. Once baby is capable of understanding mommy's feelings, you can explain that the mess makes you unhappy and you need for her to concentrate her efforts on eating instead of playing. If baby persists, just move her away from the table and end the meal. She'll learn eventually that you won't allow certain activities with food.

Baby will reach a stage when she desperately wants to hold her own spoon. Let her practice feeding herself. It will be very, very messy, so I don't recommend trying it with pureed carrots or any orange vegetables because they're the worst stainers. Try mashing bananas in a bowl, leaving convenient little clumps that will be easy for baby to scoop. If you use prepared baby food, mix in a little dry baby cereal so it's lumpier. After age one, egg salad is great because it's just clumpy enough to stay well on the spoon.

Starches are generally baby's favorites. Meats and veggies were more tricky in our family until I discovered a fabulous invention: the good old Crock-Pot—also known as a slow-cooker. In the morning you just throw in some chicken or meat (bought already chopped up), vegetables (frozen work fine), and canned tomatoes, chicken broth, or water. Season creatively, turn the thing on, and that night you have a great dinner for everyone!

I swear, there is no way to do this wrong, and you can vary the ingredients for a different stew every night. The best part is that everything turns out tasty as well as mushy, so all you have to do is lay out an assortment of pieces of vegetables and meat on baby's tray. (If baby is not eating finger foods yet, dump some stew in the blender.) I could get Tucker to eat almost anything this way. The consistency was just right for gumming, and the seasonings improved the taste immensely. (Babies shouldn't have too much salt, so let grown-ups add salt at the table.)

49.

Teach your baby to expect happiness.

Many psychologists believe that happiness is a learned condition. Babies who spend much of their time during their first years of life in a state of unhappiness will learn that unhappiness is the normal way for them to feel. We all know adults who repeatedly create unhappy situations for themselves. These people seem not to know how to be happy. Most likely, that pattern developed in their infancy. We all subconsciously seek that which is familiar, whether we consciously want to or not.

If we keep our babies as happy as possible when they are babies, they will come to think of happiness as the normal way to feel. These babies are the ones who grow up to become people who create satisfying situations and relationships for themselves and who are able to stay positive even during trying times. Which kind of adult do you want your child to become?

Besides, parenting an unhappy child is hard, frustrating work for *you*. Keeping your baby happy while he's a baby will go a long way toward making your parenting role a happy one for years to come.

Research has shown that attachment-parented babies who are carried in slings, breastfed on cue, and sleep with their parents typically cry for less than half the number of total minutes than do detachment-parented babies, who are kept in carriers, fed according to schedules, and forced to sleep alone. The longer a baby cries, the more stressed and out-of-control he gets, and the more accustomed he grows to the state of unhappiness.

Because attachment parenting minimizes stress-producing situations, attachment-parented infants are typically calm and content. And even better benefits show up later in babyhood. By the time they reach their first birthdays, attachment-parented babies cry less than one quarter as much as their detachment-parented peers! Clearly, these babies have come to recognize happiness as their normal emotional state.

I've had the privilege of witnessing firsthand the long-term effects of attachment parenting, and they are nothing short of magical. Without exception, the older children I know who were attachment-parented are warm, self-assured individuals who are clearly at ease with themselves and enjoying their lives. They are smart, funny, and popular both with their peers and with adults. They are exactly the kind of kids we all dream of having. Hey, they're the kind of people we all dream of being.

Of all the things you plan to teach your child, what could be more important than the art of happiness?

50.

Un-frustrate your mobile baby.

Once baby is mobile, the most likely reason he'll cry is frustration over his inability to use his unfolding skills as much as he'd like—and anger at you for stopping him. Babies have a burning desire to explore and learn and also no capacity for understanding that certain situations put them, as well as people's belongings, in danger.

The flashing pictures and funny noises coming from your laptop are intriguing, and baby wants to touch. You stop him, and he gets mad. He does not understand why you won't let him explore this wonderful toy. Moments later he won't remember that you wouldn't let him, and he'll probably try again. This drives you batty, but it drives baby batty too. He is just as frustrated as you are! He is not trying to manipulate you, nor is he purposely not minding you. He is merely acting out his innate need to learn. Distraction, once again, is your best strategy for keeping baby safe and nondestructive while removing him from a potentially disastrous situation.

Frustrate baby as little as possible by baby-proofing your house and scattering around lots of interesting things that he *can* explore. I like to rotate the scattered objects frequently, so that every day is a new adventure. Once he's crawling around, don't just hand baby a new object to play with. Let him find it on his own. A rinsed-out plastic ketchup bottle with a penny inside for noise value once kept seven-month-old Tuck intrigued for the better half of a morning!

Sometimes, even without your interference, baby will be frustrated by his inability to do something. It's important to let babies try to do things on their own, but there's nothing wrong with helping them out if the task being attempted is something they will obviously fail at. A baby who is trying desperately to climb a table leg to retrieve the stuffed animal hanging over the edge of the table will appreciate a lift so that he can reach the toy. If, on the other hand, baby is just learning to crawl and the stuffed animal is only slightly out of reach on the floor, it is better to wait a few minutes to see if baby will cover the ground on his own. He'll be more thrilled when he gets hold of the toy that way and will feel a boost of confidence over his achievement.

51.

Help baby become emotionally expressive.

Your child will learn to express her emotions freely if you consistently acknowledge her feelings and empathize with her. When she is an infant, responding promptly to her cues will give her the message that her wants and desires count.

When she is an older baby, her emotions will often seem unwarranted to you, like when she crumples to the ground, wailing dramatically because you won't hand her the fascinating garden shears she sees you using. It would be easy to dismiss her despair and say, "Don't be so silly. Play with this nice toy instead." But by brushing her off, you are discounting her very real feelings.

Even if you feel she *is* wrong to be so upset, try to put yourself in her shoes. She has a powerful, built-in drive to learn about the new things she sees, including the garden shears. If you take the time to help her deal with her feelings, she will feel validated. She will know that her emotions are valuable and that she is valuable. Get down to her level, look her in the eyes, and say, "You really want to play with the garden shears, don't you? It's hard when we want something and we can't have it. I won't let you play with the shears because they are sharp and might hurt you. Let's find something else that will be fun to play with."

You'll get her past the upset much more quickly this way, and her whole mood is likely to improve because even though she was denied the shears, she was made to feel understood and special in your eyes, which is what she wants and needs more than any plaything.

Always pay attention when your older baby or toddler tries to tell you something. Even if recognizable language is still months away, if you look your baby in the eyes, nod sympathetically, and try your hardest to interpret her communications, you will be surprised at the level of understanding the two of you can reach.

52.

Encourage baby to be her own person.

Even in the very first year, babies begin forming the self-image that will stick with them for life. Much of this self-image comes from you. Often babies have distinct natures right from birth, but be careful about labeling your baby as "quiet and shy" or "brave and adventurous"—or any label that might limit or inhibit your child from developing her full potential.

At around eight to ten months, baby begins to know she is a separate person with her own wishes and desires, and she begins to loudly voice her newfound will. A real sense of independence probably won't surface though until around twelve to eighteen months, when baby will do things with the specific intent of getting a reaction from you.

She'll be delighted to repeat any action that makes you laugh or praise her, but unfortunately, she may also feel compelled to repeat actions that get a negative response. She's not trying to be bad; it's all just part of the experimentation process. She may know that you said no once, but how can she know if you will always say no unless she tries it a few dozen more times?

In the first half of the second year, she'll gain the skills to work out solutions to problems, use tools to achieve goals, think of and name things she can't see at the time, and even imagine and pretend. She's begun the process of inventing herself. Though this period does represent a crucial time for establishing rules and enforcing them, try to keep restrictions to a minimum. Unless you are sensitive to baby's burgeoning sense of self, you may unwittingly nip the early buds of personality traits you later would have come to treasure in her.

53.

Help baby through the unhappy diapering phase.

At some point after eight months old, many babies become wiggle-worms on the changing table. I had a song reserved for diaper changes that usually put a halt to Tuck's protests. But sometimes the song wasn't enough and I could barely hold him down.

Start every diaper change expecting the best. If you're happy and playful and give baby a toy to distract him, he might not fuss as readily as he would if he senses that you expect him to start fussing. A particularly effective distraction is a helium balloon hovering over the diapering site, the string dangling just low enough for baby to pull on the string as the changing takes place. (Never let babies play with balloons unsupervised since they pose safety risks. Babies can choke on pieces of broken balloons or get strings over 7 inches long caught around their necks.)

My friend Jaimie lets eight-month-old Emily open and close the wipes box and pull out one or two. This treat, reserved for changing time, amuses Emily enough to keep any thought of protest at bay.

Using positive reinforcement, my friend Julie was able to psych-out a squirmy nine-month-old Luke. She explains, "I began praising Luke for being so cheerful and accommodating while I was changing him. We even applauded after every diaper change, and I made a point of thanking him for helping. It worked! Not the first time, not the twentieth time, but after about a week, he became a partner in the diaper-changing process. If I were to advise another mommy, I'd encourage her to start thanking her baby and praising proper diaper etiquette long before diaper changes become an Olympic event!"

54.

Take baby with you when you travel.

Many new parents lament the loss of the pick-up-and-go lifestyles they enjoyed before baby entered the picture. But when you practice attachment parenting, vacationing as a threesome can be almost as carefree! While most babies do relish routine, it's easy to keep attachment-parented babies happy while traveling by giving them a full measure of their favorite familiars: your body, your voice, and plenty of your loving attention. If you keep baby close to you and are sensitive to her needs, the new, exciting stimuli will likely be a treat for her.

Air travel is free for children under the age of two who are held in your arms. If there's room on the plane, some airlines will let you place baby's car seat in the seat adjacent to yours and then strap her in. Some even offer discounted fares to entice you to buy a seat to be occupied by the car seat. The airlines claim that it's safer for baby to ride strapped into a car seat, because in extreme turbulence she could fly out of your arms. I chose not to worry about that possibility because I had Tucker strapped securely to my body in the sling, where he was much happier than if he'd have been in a car seat the entire flight. (I'm not so much advising you on this point as sharing my own experience. Whether or not to put baby in her own seat on a plane is a personal decision.)

Whenever possible, plan plane rides to coincide with baby's nap times; the movement and rumble of the engine help babies doze off. If you have baby in your lap, nurse on the way up and down (or if you aren't nursing, give baby a bottle or pacifier to suck on) to alleviate pressure on tiny eardrums due to altitude change. Every breastfed baby I know sleeps peacefully on planes while nursing.

If you're flying with a toddler, give her an opportunity to run around (closely supervised!) in the airport before you board the plane, so she'll work off some energy and be ready to cuddle and relax on board. Bring new books and soft, quiet toys, and request a bulkhead seat so you'll have room for lap games. Some airlines serve baby food or crackers on request.

If you're traveling a great distance, a direct flight might not be the best way to go. A stopover will give baby a change of scenery, a chance for a comfortable diaper change, and for an older baby, an opportunity to run around.

Train travel is great for babies! It affords you a rare opportunity to give your total attention to baby without interruption from phone calls or other demands on your time. If your baby is past her first birthday, she'll likely be fascinated by the train station and also the trains themselves. Take advantage of the scenery passing outside the window for pointing out new sights and teaching baby new words. Bring books as well as soft toys you can play with together.

Even lengthy car travel can be a lot of fun for everyone as long as you have at least one other driver along. But don't expect baby to sit happily in the backseat alone. Whoever isn't driving needs to be playing with baby in the back, and if that person is the nursing mommy, all the better! My friend Amy has made several cross-country car trips with her husband, Steve, and baby Stephanie. Steve drives, Amy breastfeeds Stephanie in the car seat, and everyone talks and sings and has a great time. One advantage to car travel is the opportunity to play your own music (or baby's) and to sing or play as loudly as you like. Car sunshades help to keep baby comfortable in hot weather.

Staying in hotels is easy with a breastfeeding, co-sleeping baby. Baby is not likely to mind the unfamiliar surroundings if she's sleeping in a king-size bed between her very familiar parents. And if you're nursing, you won't have to worry about how to warm formula or baby food. If baby is eating solid foods, travel with some convenient snacks to supplement the nursing.

It's always a good idea to pack an extra bag with a day's worth of stuff in case of lost luggage. And if baby has any allergies or chronic medical conditions, before you leave find out if your doctor will handle medical problems by phone or give a local referral.

You know your baby best—keep her preferences in mind when choosing your destinations. Any environment with a comfortable temperature and activities that allow you to carry baby in the sling with you is a winner with infants. Toddlers enjoy the chance to toddle but otherwise aren't as demanding about their entertainment as they will be when they're preschoolers.

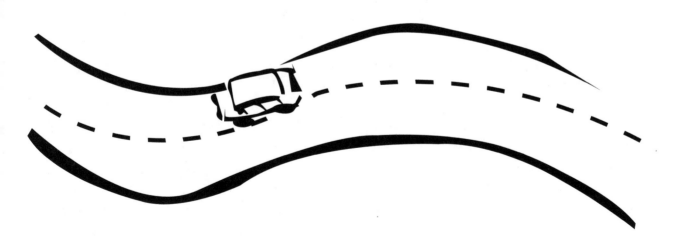

55.

Be there through the rough spots!

When your darling, sweet child suddenly turns sour and grumbly for what appears to you to be no reason at all, crank up your mothering. Your first inclination may be to give the little grump some space—and yourself a needed break—but that will actually prolong the agony.

Growing is very hard work, and the natural growth process will now and then be more than your child can comfortably handle. During these high-stress times, he needs extra cuddling, extra playtime with you, extra nursing, and extra love. Moving *toward* your child will help him get over a rough spot quickly and healthily, whereas moving *away* from him will only intensify his stress and also make it last longer.

Remember, too, that your baby is very sensitive to *your* stress level. If something in your life causes you to be less available to your baby (emotionally or physically), don't be surprised if baby's temperament changes too. Instead of blaming him for his crabby behavior, try to understand that he just misses your attention and needs reassurances you are still there for him.

56.

Be a thrifty toy shopper.

Your baby does not need a lot of toys. For the first year, every single object baby comes into contact with is something fascinating to explore and learn from, including whatever household items you give her the opportunity to examine. And if you're like many new families, you'll find that toys are filling up your home without any help from you! Plenty of parents never get the opportunity to select toys for their babies once all the relatives and friends have satisfied their gift-giving impulses.

But if somehow you find yourself without playthings for baby and she seems bored with all of your household gadgets, check out your local thrift and consignment shops. Baby certainly won't know the difference between secondhand playthings and the latest toys from a pricey store, and your toy budget will stretch a lot farther. The best playthings are the basic, traditional ones that baby can manipulate herself, like balls, blocks, and stacking toys. Look for wood or plastic standbys that offer plenty of pushing, pulling, and turning features. Keep it simple. Baby may be intrigued by complicated battery-operated toys when she sees them perform, but the more a toy does on its own, the less there is for baby to do—and the less opportunity for learning.

Blocks in particular provide an exceptional array of learning opportunities. They offer young babies the chance to practice fine-motor skills and older ones an invitation to imagine and create, building confidence and competence with every block placed. They foster an awareness of size and shape, gravity and balance, and cause and effect. *Child* magazine points out that math and science form the foundation of block constructions. Plus, blocks enrich pretend play and even enhance the development of language skills.

Balls of various sizes, too, are fascinating to babies for different reasons at different ages. A simple activity like repeatedly rolling a ball back and forth with baby forms new neural connections in baby's brain, helping it grow and giving baby the satisfaction of intentionally causing an effect in his world. In one study, an eleven-month-old joyfully rolled a ball to a caregiver 180 times before losing interest in the game. I've found inexpensive Ping-Pong balls to be a favorite for the toddler set once throwing skills kick in. They're easy for little hands to grab and throw and light enough to keep damage to a minimum. Buy extra and always keep a few stashed away for the day when all those balls that have dotted the house for weeks find their final resting places beneath your refrigerator.

When you bring toys home from thrift or consignment stores, you'll want to wash them for your own peace of mind. If you've steered clear of battery-operated toys, you'll probably be able to dump the whole haul into the upper rack of your dishwasher (plush and soft toys can usually be washed in the washing machine). It's a good idea to do this periodically with all of your baby's toys anyway, particularly if your child or a visiting child has been sick.

Some mommies are squeamish about buying clothes from thrift stores, but I see no reason not to as long as you wash the items before baby wears them. Babies often outgrow clothes long before they show any wear and tear, and you may find really adorable, quality stuff you would have never shelled out full price for in a department store. Any major equipment, though, must be checked out to make sure it's up to the latest safety standards.

As your baby outgrows toys and clothes, if you don't know a younger child to give them to and don't plan on saving them for your next addition to the family, bring them to a consignment shop. Low prices, coupled with the trade-in value of your old stuff, make it easy to have an ever evolving rotation of playthings to keep baby happily interested in learning and taking on new challenges.

57.

Don't underestimate the consequences of too little loving attention.

Babies need loving attention so much that an absence of it creates a host of negative behaviors as they grow. Attention-deprived children may become either excessively clingy or emotionally withdrawn preschoolers.

If a parent is responsive to a child only when the child is happy and perfectly behaved, that child may learn to stifle all negative feelings to ensure the parent's attention and approval—but those stifled feelings may later surface in frightening ways. These children learn to hide their emotions at home, but then may act aggressively in school, seeking from peers and teachers the response they subconsciously believe they deserve: rejection.

Babies who are deprived of loving touch may later, as children, get grimy and grubby a lot just so that a caregiver will wash them or get hurt frequently so that someone will physically tend to their boo-boos. Children can even become ill from a subconscious craving for hands-on attention from their parents. They gladly trade wellness for the touch of a hand checking their cheek or forehead for a temperature, or for the extra hugs and cuddles a sick child warrants.

When touch-deprived children reach adolescence, many become sexually promiscuous in an attempt to satisfy a still unfulfilled need for human contact. They'll likely be unable to establish emotional attachments with their lovers, however, since they will have long ago set up defenses to protect themselves from further rejection.

Drugs are another danger zone for adolescents with unfulfilled needs, subconsciously seeking parallels between the bliss of human contact and the flow of pleasurable sensations that drug use promises. And the prevalence of violence among our country's adolescents is likely due to the same root problem. In *The Vital Touch,* Sharon Heller, Ph.D., cites a study done by James Prescott—a neuropsychologist formerly with the National Institute of Child Health and Human Development of the U.S. Department of Health, Education, and Welfare—concluding that the principal cause of human violence is "a lack of bodily pleasure derived from touching and stroking during the formative periods of life."

58.

Make up songs for baby!

Create your own personal songs about diaper-changing time, car travel time, bath time, whatever. Set your own words to familiar tunes like "Twinkle, Twinkle, Little Star," "London Bridge Is Falling Down," or "Mary Had a Little Lamb." If you always sing the same song with the corresponding activity, baby will not only enjoy the activity more, but he'll also know what's in store as soon as you start singing. It's one more way to pave those early communication pathways with baby—and also provide a creative exercise for mommy's brain, in danger of atrophy from too much repetition of traditional songs and nursery rhymes (that make no sense today anyway).

Since the day my brother discovered that the letters in Tucker's name fit perfectly into the Mickey Mouse Club theme song, we've had lots of fun with variations on Disney's original lyrics. "Who's the boy who loves to eat his vegetables . . . pick up his toys . . . lie still for his diaper change . . . (you get the picture) T-U-C-K-E-R . . . "

Tuck's first word after *Mama* and *Dada* was *boom,* a word from Dada's special song for him. He used it to request a singing-and-dancing session. By the time he was a year old, the same request had morphed into a precious side-to-side swaying motion while he trilled, "La, la, la . . ." He was remarkably in tune as he repeated the first three notes of this then favorite song of his. He would get louder and louder until someone got the hint and started singing with him.

My friend Reyna sings the most adorable song for her baby, Charly (and for Tucker too), whenever a small boo-boo happens. The tempo and rhyming pattern of the song instantly captivate the little victim, and nine times out of ten he stops crying about the boo-boo so he can listen to the song. I would offer you the words to this magic remedy, but they're Spanish. The beginning translates loosely into something like "Get better, get better, you little frog's hiney," which doesn't sound nearly as poetic in English.

59.

Play music for baby.

Baby will love your voice best, but playing recorded music can be a great source of comfort and fun too. When Tucker was a newborn, he would respond dramatically to the Enya CD I had listened to throughout my pregnancy. Whenever he was tense or crying, within the first few notes, his whole little body would relax against me. As an older infant, he would visibly brighten when I played music, and as a toddler he never fails to jump up and dance when he hears a catchy beat—whether of a TV commercial or the *ch-ch, ch-ch, ch-ch* of a fax coming in!

Music is used in many hospitals to promote weight gain in preemies and also to help children recover from injuries and chemotherapy treatments. Don Campbell's book *The Mozart Effect,* tells about a tape of lullabies produced by Terry Woodford that echo the sound of a human heartbeat, used to calm infants and small children and help them sleep. Of course, an actual human heartbeat works even better—but for those babies who are forced to fall asleep alone, it is encouraging that music can deliver such great results.

Campbell writes that Woodford initially "gave away tapes to 150 day care centers, but several hospitals also obtained copies and put them to the test. At Helen Keller Hospital in Alabama, an experiment with fifty-nine newborns found that 94 percent of crying babies immediately fell asleep without a bottle or pacifier when exposed to the music. At the University of Alabama at Birmingham, nurses used the *Baby-Go-to-Sleep* tape for infants recovering from open heart surgery. One baby, struggling on a respirator, was near death when desperate nurses turned to Terry's tape. To their astonishment, the baby calmed down, fell asleep, and lived." Woodford went on to give away thousands more tapes, which are used widely in neonatal intensive-care units all over the country. You can purchase one by calling (719) 473-0100.

60.

Research your human heritage.

As I've stressed throughout this book, you do know exactly how you are meant to relate to your baby. Our biological makeup has equipped us with all the right instincts to meet our babies' needs. The trick is to fully trust our instincts and disregard the notions of a society that has gone far astray in its child-rearing practices.

One of the best ways to reinforce these instincts is to research the human animal. If I had the chance to affect the whole world by passing a single law, I would make Jean Liedloff's classic book *The Continuum Concept* required reading for every expectant parent. Please, please, *please* buy this book and read it! The author studied and lived with the native population deep in the South American jungle, whose way of life today closely resembles that of prehistoric humans. Liedoff's findings about human nature are so completely astounding, and yet so recognizably right, that once you have read her book you will never look at your baby the same way again.

Oversimplified, the premise is that every living creature is born with a hardwired set of expectations, or instincts, to facilitate its survival. For millions of years, human babies were breastfed on cue, slept next to their mothers, and were carried constantly. The survival of our species depended on it. Only in the last few thousand years—a nanosecond in the grand scheme of evolution—have things been any different. A few thousand years isn't nearly enough time to change the hardwiring of a species, so our babies are born expecting the same sensory stimuli our ancestors received.

This is why babies behave the way they do. They are born expecting to be carried by active adults, so they are soothed when you hold them and walk with them. Our distant ancestors had plenty of foraging and working to do while wearing baby, and baby expects that kind of activity from you! It's not just that babies want to be nurtured in this way—they crave it from their innermost beings. Any deviation from their hardwired expectations is terrifying—a threat to their very survival. For our ancestors to have left a helpless baby all alone would have meant death for that baby in the jaws of predators.

Babies today are born with that same instinctive need for the sustaining shelter of human contact. Being left alone triggers a barrage of stress hormones. They cry out as if they are terrified, and their terror is very real. These intuitive little creatures are reminding us that we are not fulfilling our roles as human parents. They're giving us clear and recognizable signals, and we as a society are ignoring them because some of our recent "experts" have advised us that it is normal and healthy for babies to be left to cry.

Back in the 1930s, anthropologist Margaret Mead observed two New Guinea tribes, the Arapesh and the Mundugumor. The Arapesh were loving, peaceful people who carried their babies against their bodies, nursed them until they initiated weaning, and treated them with respect and playful affection. The babies seldom cried, and if one did, he would be immediately comforted at his mother's breast. Generation after generation, the Arapesh enjoyed a beautifully functioning society.

The Mundugumor were openly aggressive and hostile with one another and with surrounding tribes. Their babies were kept in hard, stiff baskets and received little contact with their caregivers. When a baby cried, his mother would scratch the outside of the basket to silence him. Babies were held only enough to provide adequate nourishment for their survival, then returned to the baskets. As one would expect, these babies grew to fit perfectly into their culture, which was a violent, disjointed one, notorious for warring and head-hunting.

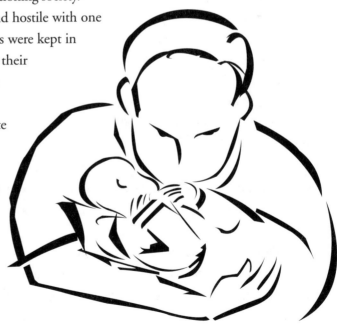

Our contemporary society offers many lifestyles to choose from. How you raise your baby now will influence the lifestyle she will one day select for herself.

61.

Remember, babies live in the present moment.

Lack of sensory stimulation is just one of the agonies millions of babies endure because their mothers have lost touch with their primal instincts. Another is a feeling of abandonment. When babies' needs are not met and their cries ignored, there is simply no way for them to be spared some degree of psychological damage.

You may be thinking, "But what about my cousin's baby? I know she lets him cry alone in his crib at night, and every time I see him he's smiling and laughing. He seems so happy and well-adjusted." The fact that the fallout from a baby's unfulfilled needs may not be apparent for several years is one of the most troubling features of detached parenting. I've listed some long-term effects elsewhere in this book: the lack of self-esteem, the difficulty in communicating, and forming relationships with others. But on a short-term basis, the detachment-parented baby may seem very happy when in the company of others. After all, babies have no concept of blame or even of time. The moment they are experiencing is the only moment they know.

Jean Liedloff explains that well-intentioned but detached mothers have no idea how poorly they are treating their children because the deprived babies figure out that smiling is one way to get the attention they so badly crave. "Because he smiles encouragingly whenever she comes to him, his mother is convinced that she is the appreciated mother of a happy baby. The bitter ordeal that is all the rest of his waking life does not create any negative feeling toward her; on the contrary, it makes him all the more desperate to be with her."

Babies desperate to be held and nurtured will soon learn to repeat any behavior that helps them achieve that desired end. They may even appear happier than attachment-parented babies when with others because the experience is such a welcome and wonderful contrast to the rest of their bleak lives.

62.

Make dressing time fun for baby.

Some babies hate the feeling of air against their bare skin. Others love it so much that they hate having clothes put on them. The same baby might even go through stages where one, then the other of the above statements describe him! Most parents can expect to experience at least one phase in their child's babyhood when dressing time is no fun.

Obviously, the more comfortable your baby's clothes, the more he will enjoy wearing them. Very young babies need wide necks or snaps because their little pumpkin heads are so darn big for their bodies! Having a shirt pulled over their faces is scary stuff for infants, so talk soothingly and give up immediately on any garment that doesn't easily slide over the head. The comfiest choices for young babies are cotton bodysuits that go on bottom first.

When baby is a little older, it's easy to make up games to accompany dressing. As the shirt goes over his head you say, "Where is Nicholas? I don't see my Nicholas!" Then as his head pops through, "There's Nicholas!" Or as you work a hand through a sleeve, "Where is Nicholas's hand?" Once again, songs made up for the occasion can go a long way toward making dressing time a fun time.

Think through your game plan before you begin. For example, if the garment has snaps at the crotch and also down the front, the best plan might be to snap all the crotch snaps in advance, then slide baby in feet-first. Even with the distraction of songs or games, you may have to work lightening-fast to finish before baby starts protesting. For some reason, "Oops!" always bought me some time. If Tuck started squirming, I could pretend to drop a sock and exclaim "Oops!" in exchange for a laugh that would last just long enough to get that last button fastened.

If you live in a warm climate—or at least have a warm season where you live—let baby try out nakedness, indoors and out! This allows for more skin-to-skin contact (particularly if you're willing to go around scantily clad yourself) and also gives baby the chance to feel the warmth of the sun (for brief periods!) and the caress of the wind. Most parents will opt for at least a diaper, though my friend Kathleen lets her toddler, Cullen, enjoy the backyard completely au naturel, much to Cullen's delight. If she tries to leave a diaper on, he indignantly does his best to remove it.

Shoes are particularly bothersome to some new walkers, especially since it's hard for a parent to tell if a particular shoe is comfortable for a child. My pediatrician says there's no need for those specially-designed-for-babies orthopedic shoes that cost a bundle. He and many other docs feel that barefoot is best unless baby is walking around outside where his feet need protection. Then any shoe that's flexible and comfortable will do just fine. I've got to believe that Mother Nature's pretty good at this stuff. She probably built baby's feet in such a way that his walking talents would unfold best if her design was left alone.

63.

Stay focused on the big picture.

There will be many times in your baby's first few years when his demands on you will seem overwhelming and you will feel impossibly imposed upon. It's tempting in these moments to take parenting shortcuts for their promise of temporary relief. Don't fall for these traps! As terminal as the condition may seem, your baby will outgrow this incessantly demanding phase. Babies have huge needs! The only way to help them need you less in the long run is to meet those needs fully as they arise.

There will be times when even a toddler will need to be constantly in your arms. If you consent, he will be reassured and soon be off on his own again. However, if you refuse, the need will intensify. He'll be more clingy and more whiny until you both go crazy or until you finally give in and provide the intensive parenting he craves.

As the well-known child psychologist Lee Salk has shown repeatedly in his research, needs that are satisfied go away. Those that are not, remain, but may appear different as the child grows. Dependency in infancy is natural and healthy. But children who are deprived of the opportunity to be happily dependent never mature into happy independence. Their dependencies become the unhealthy kind we're so used to seeing in older children and adults.

Training a baby to keep quiet in a room all by himself all night is an example of denying him the dependency he requires. Forcing a baby to wean from the breast before he is ready and leaving him with a substitute caregiver before he has had time to bond with her are other examples. These things seem—on the surface—to make life easier for the parent, but in the long run, they make a parent's job much, much harder!

Babies who have been rushed into independence are the ones who become angry and aggressive toddlers. Once they reach two years old, their behavior is explained away as typical of the "terrible twos." Dr. William Sears calls these negative traits "diseases of premature weaning" and stresses that they are not exhibited by all two-year-olds. He states: "In my twenty-two years of pediatric practice I have noticed that the most well-behaved children are those that were not weaned before their time." His usage of the word "weaned" applies not only to breastfeeding, but to all forms of attached parenting.

Listen to your baby and make attending to him a priority. Whining in a child is a direct consequence of a parent's failure to respond attentively to him. It usually occurs after a child has made several straightforward requests for attention that have been rebuffed, or if he has become so used to being rebuffed that he has turned to chronic whining and it is now second nature to him.

There is simply no consequence-free way to avoid investing an enormous amount of your time and energy early on into raising your child. But the attention you give your child in the first few years will guarantee you enormous paybacks in the years to come! Giving your time freely and lovingly during the years your baby needs it most sets up an insurance policy for happier parenting throughout the rest of his childhood.

64.

Keep a bag of tricks for getting baby out of a funk.

Every baby is going to be in a funk now and then. Don't bad moods creep up on *you* from time to time? Don't you love it when someone important to you knows just how to cheer you up? Every parent should keep a little arsenal of weapons against that dreaded visitor, inexplicable baby-angst.

For very young babies, nursing and carrying baby in the sling will usually do the trick. But for times when they don't, your arsenal might include a particular song, a walk around the yard, or a special way of holding her. My best friend, Christina, was having a hard time comforting her infant, Jessica, when Christina's brother, Lars, was inspired with the perfect solution. He took his little niece through the house on a smelling tour! A baby's sense of smell is highly developed, and Lars found that opening jars of pickles or ketchup bottles and offering them for Jessica to sniff distracted her from her crying. Christina used smelling tours often after that first experiment and they always worked!

For older babies, toys and objects they haven't seen before often provide a quick fix. Members of the newly toddling set are easily distracted by almost any new gadget as long as it's sufficiently intriguing. My friend Sara is a veritable Felix the Cat, never failing to produce from the recesses of her handbag some spectacular rubber dinosaur or similarly fascinating object, much to the delight of her daughter, Carly, and Tucker too.

Tuck's grandma scored big points one day with Tic Tacs. The container is the perfect size and shape for tiny hands to hold; Tic Tacs look and sound really cool when shaken, and best of all, babies can smell and almost taste the minty treats by sucking on the plastic top. (Watch baby with Tic Tacs! Make sure the container is tightly sealed and remove the paper label if you don't want your baby to eat it.) My husband's favorite standby is a pen light. Tuck is fascinated by his ability to turn it on and off as well as by the effects he can create by shining it on the floor or walls.

When you find yourself with an unhappy baby and no props, question baby excitedly about his latest accomplishment. At around fourteen to fifteen months, Tucker never failed to cheer up when I would ask him, "Can Tucker make a LOUD noise?" Even if he had been crying, he would stop, smile, and show me just how loud he could be. The natural follow-up question was, "Now can Tucker make a QUIET noise?" He'd grin conspiratorially and give me his best whisper. Naming body parts is another fun game to play when you're stuck without any toys, and my husband is always able to conquer the crabbies by flying Tuck over his head, airplane-style.

Figuring out what floats her boat is part of bonding with your baby. Experiment, and through trial and error, create baby's personal list of favorite things. Then try your best to fill her world with them—especially on those days when she's blue and needs a little extra love.

65.

Don't hoard baby's love all for yourself.

The second half of baby's first year is when the attachments he has already begun to form become really strong. Most often the mother is the primary attachment figure, but it could be a father or other caregiver. It is usually the person the baby spends the most time with and gets the most attention from. But moms who worry that baby will get too attached to a hired caregiver at the exclusion of attaching himself to her shouldn't be concerned. Babies have an unlimited amount of love to give. As long as mom makes an effort to be a special part of baby's life, baby will love her.

And even when mom is the primary caregiver, it is nice for baby to have an extended circle of special people to love. It makes it easier for mom to have occasional breaks from baby and know baby is happy. And special people don't have to be family members. Tuck lives several thousand miles away from his beloved Auntie Aimee, but he has enjoyed a special bond with his substitute auntie, my friend Cheryl, since his birth. Even during his most anxious period of separation anxiety, Auntie Cheryl was always met with a smile and open arms.

New mommies tend to make friends with other new mommies because new-mommy-ness is such a huge and overwhelming condition that it can make women who would otherwise have little in common suddenly feel like soul sisters. But a babyless buddy, like our Cheryl, can be a real asset too, as long as she's a fraction as in love with your baby as you are.

Occasionally talking about non-baby-related issues can feel like a fascinating break for a baby-brained new mom. Plus, when you want to go somewhere with a babyless friend, there's only one baby's erratic nap schedule to factor in. You can get together even if your baby is sick (mommy-friends won't come within miles of you and your sick baby). When you go to the mall during holiday season, you only have one stroller full of shopping bags to maneuver through the crowds, and a ratio of two adults to one baby means there's always someone to hold the door open, to drive, and to play peekaboo.

66.

See if you can nip colic in the bud.

Statistics indicate that 20 percent of American babies suffer from colic, which means you have a one-in-five chance of having a colicky baby. But what is colic? Generally, any baby who cries for more than three hours a day, at least three days a week, for three straight weeks is labeled colicky, especially during the period between two weeks and three months of age.

The very fact that we have a name for this circumstance implies that our culture considers colic a familiar condition. But in cultures outside our own, there is no word for *colic,* and its symptoms are unknown to parents who don't subscribe to our contemporary Western child-rearing practices. In cultures where mothers and babies are rarely apart, babies rarely cry at all.

It seems that we ourselves have created the colicky infant. Why, then, don't more American babies suffer? Researchers have speculated that while all babies crave continual, loving contact with a caregiver who responds promptly to their cues, some are just more adamant about having that need met than others.

No matter what baby's natural temperament is, attachment-parented babies are far less likely to get stamped with the colic label. Here's why: Colic has been associated with digestive problems, and babies who eat and spend most of their time in an upright position (held babies) are less likely to have gas than are babies generally fed in a reclined or semireclined position. Plus, breastfed babies have far fewer digestive problems than do bottlfed babies. And studies have shown that being held tummy-to-tummy actually helps babies' stomachs perform better—as if the parent's tummy is teaching baby's what to do!

Another significant cause of gas is swallowed air from the act of crying itself. Babies who are comforted immediately—before their crying gets out of control—are therefore less likely to form painful gas bubbles.

Could the immediate response to baby's cries be the answer to the colic problem? Mommies in a mothers' group I attended were lamenting the hours they spent walking the floor with their colicky babies. One of my attachment-parenting friends asked these moms how quickly they picked up their babies once they began to cry. All admitted that they waited for several minutes in the hopes their babies would settle down. My friend tactfully suggested that they try picking up their babies at the first whimper, just to see if it would make a difference.

It did! The moms who started picking up their babies right away found they were able to prevent the crying from escalating to that point-of-no-return wailing that tormented them for weeks.

A conclusion could be drawn that some babies just have a lower tolerance for inattentiveness from their caregivers than others do. Once these babies hit their thresholds, if not nurtured properly they go into a rage that is nearly impossible for them to get themselves out of, even once the nurturing begins. For colicky babies, that threshold may be well under a minute!

67.

If night nursing becomes more than you can bear, let Dad step in.

Many, many parents find co-sleeping a peaceful, cozy, wonderful way to carry their daytime parenting practices into the nighttime. A small percentage, however, become disappointed by baby's enduring enthusiasm for frequent night nursing.

Most babies will nurse during the night if given the opportunity, and a few snacks are not likely to significantly disrupt anyone's sleep. (See Way 31 for an explanation of in-sync sleep cycles.) But some babies, even after their first birthdays, still frequent Mom like an all-night diner. Some moms shrug this off, knowing it will all soon be a distant memory, but others become tempted to throw in the towel on the whole co-sleeping arrangement.

If you ever find yourself a member of that second group and if baby is well beyond his six-month birthday, try letting Dad break baby of an excessive nighttime nursing habit. *Parents* magazine ran a really nice story about a family that was having a difficult time sharing sleep because of baby's all-night nursing. The eight-month-old son had come to associate nursing with sleeping and could only fall asleep when nursed. Unfortunately, he was an extremely light sleeper, as were his parents.

Sleep deprivation from being woke hourly for weeks on end forced the parents to make a change in their arrangement, but they were against any crib-training technique that required their son to "cry it out." Instead, they let Dad and baby sleep together, without Mom, for a while. Whenever baby awoke, Dad comforted him back to sleep—without much success for the first few nights, but with increasing success thereafter. This strategy served to break baby of the need to nurse to fall asleep, while still letting him feel loved and valued.

The baby began eating solid foods with much greater gusto, and after several days he was sleeping through the night. The father writes:

> I found I loved sleeping with my son. As I slipped in quietly next to him, moving his tiny feet away from my side of the bed, the band of fatherhood coiled tightly about my heart. His little face looked so trusting, sweet breath exhaling through his perfect mouth, eyelids fluttering with dreams. Sometimes one hand would reach out and grab me, tugging at the hair on my forearm, as if to reassure himself in his sleep that I was there. I kissed his forehead, and then we would sleep together, nose to nose, toe to chest. The closeness that my wife had experienced while nursing was suddenly, wonderfully, visited upon me.

What an awesome bonding experience for fathers and babies! Dr. William Sears provides more information about father nursing in his excellent books, *The Baby Book* and *Nighttime Parenting*.

While the baby in the article responded well to a cold-turkey end to his night nursings, another approach sounds even more effective to me. In *Solve Your Child's Sleep Problems,* Dr. Richard Ferber outlines a plan to reduce night nursing slowly so that the child won't experience hunger (since she is accustomed to consuming lots of calories during the night). The idea is to nurse baby only once every two hours the first night, once every two-and-one-half hours the second night, once every three hours the third night, and so on until baby becomes accustomed to not nursing during night hours. (I do not recommend any other part of Dr. Ferber's regimen, however, since the goal of his book is for baby to be alone throughout the night which is not at all the goal here.)

So I'm suggesting a combination of the above two solutions, whereby baby lessens night nursings gradually, with Mom returning to nurse him at the appropriate intervals (only if baby wakes up), and Dad sleeps with baby and pitches in with any comforting that's necessary in between. By about a week, baby and Dad may be sleeping together peacefully through the night, at which point Mom can return for good.

68.

Help baby build muscles for developmental milestones.

Some parents are afraid that their babies won't reach developmental milestones like sitting, crawling, and walking if they spend too much time in their parents' arms. Research has proved the exact opposite. Babies who are carried most of the time (in arms or in slings) sit, stand, and walk earlier than babies who aren't.

It turns out that once again nature has provided the perfect design. The exact muscles that babies exercise when they are straddling an active human are the ones they need to develop for sitting, standing, and walking. Holding his head upright helps baby develop the balance necessary for these activities, while the extended position of his neck and back and the flexed position of his hips all build muscle strength in precisely the required areas.

In sharp contrast is the baby left to flail about in a container. The random movements baby is able to generate on his own do little to further his development. Eventually, through much trial and error, he'll figure out how to sit and walk, but not as smoothly and naturally as his carried counterpart.

Dr. T. Berry Brazelton says, "When I studied the Mayan Indians in Southern Mexico for their child-rearing patterns, I longed for the revival in our society of at least two customs that we as a culture have given up. I longed for mothers to allow themselves more continual physical closeness with their infants and for the cushioning of the extended family for all young parents."

It's not easy for a couple to carry a baby all the time, and especially hard when one parent shoulders most of the burden. That's why slings are essential and extended family so important—even if it has to be a family you yourself create with friends and neighbors and hired help. On days when you feel resentment toward your heavy little bundle, try to keep the big picture in mind. This stage won't last forever, but the rewards of raising a confident, loving, well-adjusted person certainly will!

Turn off the tube.

While there are some great educational television shows for older kids, babies under two years old don't benefit much from them. Television may seem like an ideal way to teach baby language, but studies have shown that babies don't hear words coming from a television set in the same way they hear live spoken words. Babies need human interaction to be able to pick out and separate words from one another. Television will sound like background noise to a baby and may even drown out his chance to hear real human dialogue. Visually, babies need the depth and movement of three-dimensional objects to stimulate their curiosity and help them learn. Most babies show no interest in the television anyway. Turn it off and let your interactions with your ever amazing child provide the entertainment for you both!

70.

Help baby learn language.

Before your baby can move her tongue and mouth muscles to make recognizable sounds, she already understands the meanings of many words, especially if you've been talking to her regularly since birth. You can build an impressive communication network with your baby before she begins speaking by asking questions she can answer with a nod or pointing. *Where* questions are good starters, such as "Where is Mama's nose?" Tucker could correctly identify Mama's and Dada's noses before we could get him to simply point to Mama or Dada, I suppose because the nose game was more fun for him!

Babies delight in having their attempts at communication understood. The degree to which your child will enjoy talking will depend in part on how much you encourage her early attempts.

You've probably had the experience of talking to someone who nods politely while not listening to a word you're saying. Does this reaction make you want to keep talking? Don't you much prefer talking to someone who hangs on your every word? Babies are the same way. If you watch your baby intently and make every effort to comprehend the words your little orator is delivering, you'll be rewarded with much more frequent communication attempts and a baby you can converse with at an early age.

Your baby will most likely say words incompletely or incorrectly before mastering them. Don't correct her or she may feel she's displeasing you and stop trying. It's better to just happily let her know you understand, then repeat the word back to her cheerfully and correctly. For example, baby says "Guk" as she splashes in the bathtub and you reply, "Yes, that *is* your duck! Here comes your duck! What does a duck say?" Baby sees your excitement that she correctly labeled the duck and also gets to hear it pronounced correctly a few more times in different contexts. The most important thing is for baby to realize that you understand her and that you're as thrilled with her accomplishment as she is.

Let baby take the lead. It may seem frustrating to you that her first words include such vocalizations as *quack-quack, uh-oh,* and *boom!* but it's not uncommon. Babies reproduce sounds that are fun to them. Don't worry that baby will delay learning more useful words because she's spending time on the silly ones. On the contrary, baby's incentive to add to her vocabulary will be increased by her enjoyment of the words she's chosen as her first.

Pronouns are infinitely confusing to babies who are just getting the hang of labeling things. If Mommy is sometimes "Mommy" but also sometimes "I" and sometimes "me" and sometimes "she" or "her" and even "you" if Daddy is talking to her, it's going to take a lot longer for baby to learn a label for that nice thing that is Mommy. You may feel silly doing it at first, but you'll make life easier for your baby if you always use names when talking to her. "Mommy is going to give Natalie a bath now" is easier for her to make sense of than "I'm going to give you a bath."

You might take baby for a walk around the house and notice the objects she pays the most attention to. Label these for her frequently and they'll likely show up soon in her vocabulary. Once she has a few words under her belt, encourage her to talk to people other than you. You may have to serve as interpreter until they recognize her particular versions of words, but make sure anyone caring for baby is up on the lingo so that she won't be unduly frustrated at her sudden inability to be understood.

71.

Learn to read baby's attempts at communication.

Babies are capable of the same range of emotion that adult humans are. They love and hate things just as intensely as we do. But babies have so much less control over their circumstances. That's why much of baby's crying is an attempt to signal you to do something for him. If you leave the room and baby wants to go with you, he can't tell you so, but he can cry until you get the message and come back for him. If you run into a friend who holds out his arms for baby, baby can't tell you, "I don't want to go to this person," so he cries in the hopes you will hear his concern.

Try as often as you can to tune into your baby's attempts at communication *before* he feels the need to cry. When you're about to leave the room, let baby know. Maybe he'll hold his arms up to tell you he wants to come too, and you can avoid putting him into the position to cry. Before handing him over to your friend, look to see how baby is perceiving the newcomer. You'll probably be able to tell from baby's face that a handover isn't going to please him.

Babies can understand language a lot sooner than they can form the mouth and tongue movements to speak it intelligibly. To get a realistic handle on how much baby is comprehending, think about how much of your spoken communication you believe he is understanding, *then double that.* It's frustrating for the little guy to understand you but not have the power to make you understand him. Linda Acredolo, Ph.D., and Susan Goodwyn, Ph.D., remind us, "It doesn't matter how big or little you are, successful communication with other people makes life better. In fact, for the very young and helpless it may be even more important." Their book, *Baby Signs* helps parents work out a personalized gestural language with their preverbal babies. Tuck and I used a lot of meaningful gestures before we started conversing for real. It's helpful and a lot of fun too!

72.

Dine out with baby.

If you are respectful of baby's needs, eating out isn't difficult and the change of scenery can be entertaining for her. When baby is still an infant, she may fall asleep in the car on the way to your destination. If she does and if your car seat is one that can be easily snapped out to become a carrier, take your sleeping baby into the restaurant in her carrier. Many restaurants now have holders for carriers; otherwise you can turn a high chair upside down and place the carrier on top. Bring your sling in too, in case she wakes up. You will be amazed at the level of noise some babies can sleep through. Most often it takes a sudden change in the noise level to startle baby awake.

If she wakes up fussing, transfer her to the sling and nurse her while you eat. If you've practiced with the sling ahead of time, you'll find it entirely discreet and not difficult to eat around, though I'd recommend staying away from hot soups and beverages. My friend Kathleen was eating once with her son, Cullen, nursing in the sling. He was so comfortable that he didn't even complain about the pea that kamikazied from her fork directly into his little ear, later requiring some delicate extraction. If baby starts to fuss, a walk around the restaurant or out in the parking lot may soothe her. Be prepared to pack up the meal and finish it at home if need be.

If you've taken baby out all along, she'll be used to restaurants and easier to handle in them when she's older. Many older babies enjoy sitting in restaurant high chairs more than sitting in high chairs at home because the new environment offers so much to watch. Bring along neat-but-nutritious foods like fortified cereals or bite-sized pieces of cheese, chicken, meatballs, cooked carrots, or green beans. Always have antiseptic wipes with you to wipe down the high chair.

Most babies throw dishes on the floor, so place baby's food directly on the sanitized tray or table. Or, better yet, order those handy disposable place mats. They're plastic, with tape along the underneath edges so that they stick right to the high-chair tray or tabletop. When the meal is over, you just peel them off and throw away the mess. (You can order them through Designs by Chad and Jake, 877-FUN-KIDS.) Those bowls that suction themselves to the table would seem a decent alternative, but I've never had much success with them. Tuck either figures out how to un-suction them or focuses all his energies on transferring the food out of the bowl onto the table anyway.

My dining-out-parent friends agree that babies are much happier when they can sit outdoors. That's not always possible, of course, but sitting next to a window can provide entertainment too. If you are eating outdoors in the evening, make sure baby is properly dressed for a temperature drop and if insects are present, protect baby with an age-appropriate bug repellent.

If your baby is a fidgeter, don't put her in the high chair until your meal arrives. We get a booth and let Tuck stand, dance, and walk on the seat until the food comes. Some restaurants will let you call in your order before you leave home, thereby saving you a little downtime once you arrive. And if baby is old enough for a kid's meal, ask your server to bring it ahead of the rest of the food.

73.

Explore books with baby.

Parents often feel silly reading to a very young baby, so I'll just suggest that you regularly explore books with your child. If you sit down with your baby and a book often enough, you'll find that your baby will let you know how much he's ready for—and you'll be amazed at how quickly that changes!

Books are a perfect device for teaching babies the names for things. You could start out with simple board books that have a single image and word on each page, or you could use any children's books with clear, bold illustrations and pick out things to label for baby. Baby will make connections more easily if you label both the picture version and a version of the real thing whenever you have one handy. For example, point to the ball in the book as you say "ball," and then point to the ball on the floor and say "ball." Babies naturally love to label things so you may be surprised at how soon baby can "read" these same books to you.

Don't limit book exploration to labeling, though. Start reading simple stories to your baby as soon as you sense he'll stay interested even for a few pages. Don't be offended if it takes many starts before the day he lets you finish the story—always let him determine how long the reading session should last. If you underline the text with your finger as you read, he'll eventually get the message that those black squiggly lines in his books hold the story. That concept will help him embrace learning to read when the time comes.

Make sure reading time is always pleasurable. When your baby is old enough to have preferences about things, get books that match baby's passions. If he's fascinated with the neighbor's cat, get a book about cats and intersperse your reading with lots of heartfelt meows and purrs. No matter what the book, use exaggerated voices and silly noises whenever you can. Your enthusiasm will elevate his. When he finds something you read funny, share his laughter. If you can laugh with him genuinely (fake laughs won't cut it), you'll not only enhance your own bond but also lay a firm foundation for future enjoyment of books.

74.

Help baby release pent-up stress.

Although children should never be left to cry alone, crying and raging can be beneficial if you provide the appropriate emotional support. In her groundbreaking book, *Tears and Tantrums*, Dr. Aletha J. Solter offers highly useful advice on what to do when babies and children cry. She suggests that parents should not always look for solutions to stop a child's crying. Instead, they should simply allow the child to experience ownership of her feelings and to express them fully.

Of course, any crying situation must first be assessed to make sure baby's needs are all met. But when her demands are truly unreasonable, it's time to consider the possibility that she only needs to release pent-up emotions. Babies and toddlers experience enormous stress as they adjust to their ever-changing abilities and circumstances. Crying and raging are the only mechanisms they have to release this stress. When a parent consistently blocks the crying or raging, either by succumbing to every unreasonable demand or by ignoring the child (and thereby, in effect, punishing the child), the child will assume that her emotions are wrong and will likely suppress them to please the parent. Having a child who cries less may sound convenient, but the accumulation of pent-up stress will soon render her whiny, irritable, or even sick.

It's very common for well-intentioned parents to try to keep their babies from crying. The pattern is handed down from generation to generation. If you think you may be blocking this healthy stress-release mechanism in your child, Dr. Solter recommends the following:

1. Take your crying baby into your arms, sit in a comfortable chair, and look at her face. If her eyes are open, look into her eyes. Feel her energy and life force. Hold her calmly, without bouncing or jiggling.
2. Take some deep breaths and try to relax. Be aware of the love you have for your baby.
3. Talk to your baby. Tell her, "I love you. I'm listening. You're safe with me. I will stay with you. It's okay to cry." You might also try to figure out the source of her crying while verbalizing your thoughts: "Did you have a hard day? Maybe we did too much today." Tell her that you know how hard it is to be a baby. Let her know that you want to make her feel better.

4. Be aware of your own emotions. If you need to cry with her, go right ahead. Tell her that you are sad.

5. If she arches away from you or does not look at you, tell her, "Please look at me. I'm here. I want you to feel safe with me." Gently touch your baby's arms or face to reassure her of your physical presence. Don't be surprised if this causes louder crying than before.

6. Continue to stay with your baby and hold her lovingly until she spontaneously stops crying.

When a parent follows the above steps, baby knows that it is okay for her to feel any emotions, and she learns the valuable lesson that releasing them will make her feel better. Babies need this support to be able to fully release their stress. The worst thing a parent can do when a baby cries is say "Don't cry," or any other phrase that negates the feeling or makes it inappropriate in baby's mind. Crying should never be treated as misbehavior. Even if the reason for the outburst seems completely irrational to you, the child's emotional pain is real, and is probably left over from prior incidents. Haven't you ever had a day when the built-up tension inside you is finally released over some seemingly trivial problem?

Parents often suspect that their child is turning on the tears for manipulative purposes. They resist responding lovingly because they don't want to encourage subsequent outbursts. But it is impossible, Dr. Solter claims, for a child to cry at will—unless she's storing stress she needs to release. Dr. Solter equates crying with defecating. No one ever accuses a child of defecating just to get attention, or assumes that indulging defecation will somehow make the child repeat the act more frequently. Kids will do it exactly as often as they need to, and tears work the same way.

Many parents have found that when they began offering loving support during crying and raging, their babies and toddlers became more affectionate, kind, and joyous. Aggressive behaviors, whining, and even sleep disturbances can subside! Could some of your child's less endearing traits be the result of pent-up stress that isn't being released? Try Dr. Solter's technique and find out!

75.

Indulge baby's possessiveness of you.

Even if baby has many special people accepted into his circle, by six or seven months he will probably have chosen one (usually mom) as his most desired companion. Childcare expert Penelope Leach calls this relationship baby's "first, and arguably most important, love affair." Baby will not want to let you out of his sight and will be unhappy to have to share you with anyone else.

Leach explains, "He feels passionately for you physically. He will sit on you, play with you, stroke and pull you, pop food (and worse) in your mouth, behaving as if your body belonged to him." This behavior is normal and healthy and does not indicate future behavior that is clingy and overly dependent. Many experts agree that the stronger these early attachments are, the more independent the child will eventually become, as trust in the world is the underlying necessary ingredient for confidence and self-love.

It's really helpful if you can keep that in mind while your child is going through separation anxiety because it can drive you insane. During the most intense period of separation anxiety, it can feel utterly impossible to calmly do anything for one moment by yourself. Often this phase means baby is no longer content just doing his own thing while you do your own thing in the same room. Baby wants to see exactly what you're doing UP CLOSE and he wants to HELP YOU DO IT. It's easy to become impatient with this possessive phase in baby's development, but if you can remind yourself of its transience and keep your sense of humor, you might even enjoy it. How often do we get to be on the receiving end of such overwhelming adoration?

It is so much better for baby if you can indulge and revel in this intense attachment with him. Ignoring his cries to be with you will send an unmistakably harmful message, and it won't help you out of the problem since he'll just become more and more anxious about your love. The more anxious he feels, the more determinedly he'll cling.

Don't try sneaking out on him either. Even when he seems completely engrossed in emptying and restocking your underwear drawer, resist the urge to tiptoe into the next room for one quick little switch of the stereo dial. He'll be furious when he discovers your abandonment, and then he'll occupy himself less and less because he'll know he has to keep his eyes on you at all times.

Take him with you whenever you possibly can, and when you leave him use a familiar phrase to let him know what's going on. Say something like "Be right back!" when you really will and "See you soon!" when you'll be gone longer. When you do have to leave him with someone, make sure it is someone he is also attached to. An acquaintance baby hasn't yet had the chance to bond with is not a good baby-sitter. A stranger is even worse. He simply cannot help feeling threatened in such a situation, no matter how well you know the person and how much you trust her.

As difficult as it can be to live with, separation anxiety truly is healthy and normal, and your baby's feelings are very real and legitimate. Leach says, "The baby is practicing love for life. The more he can love now, and feel himself loved back, the more generous with, and accepting of, all kinds of love he will be right through his life."

76.

Keep strangers at bay!

Given the right set of circumstances, your baby may not exhibit any stranger anxiety at all. The right set of circumstances means that you do not ever try to hand baby to a stranger, leave baby with a stranger, or force baby to kiss or hug a stranger. If all strangers keep their appropriate distance, chances are baby will smile and coo for them and genuinely enjoy meeting them.

It is when people fail to treat babies with the same respect they extend to adults that babies become anxious. Would you enjoy strangers of all shapes and sizes grabbing at you and kissing you while your husband stood by smiling and encouraging them? Penelope Leach says, "We like to know people before we accept close approaches and physical affection from them; babies feel the same, and deserve protecting from those who try to treat them like pets."

Mommies often forget that their babies aren't actually a part of themselves. (Tuck and I spent so much time glued together that I sometimes referred to him as my best feature.) We think that if we recognize and love someone, baby should too. But unless baby has spent plenty of time in the company of Aunt Gloria, she may as well be a visitor from Mars.

If you want your baby to accept someone new into his circle, put in the hours. Let baby see how much you enjoy the person and how comfortable you are in her company. Ask her to talk to and interact with baby from a distance and let baby be the one to narrow the gap when he's ready. Going at baby's pace will allow him to love her sooner than forcing her on him would.

Leach explains:

> Anxieties over being away from you and being with people who are neither you nor known friends are real fears. Like other fears they will die down most quickly in babies who are given least cause to feel them. At present your baby is too newly in love with you to take you for granted. But if you can ride him through this period of intense and potentially anxious attachment on a wave of securely returned and protective adoration, he will come to take your love and your safety for granted in the end. Only when he has had a full measure of you will he be ready for other adults and for other children. Only a ground-base of confidence in his home relationships will make him free and ready to turn his attention outward as he gets older.

77.

Minimize baby's fears.

Baby will most likely cry far less in his second six months than he did in his first and for different reasons. Baby's cries at this later time are more likely to be due to frustration or fear, and the things that make him afraid may appear totally irrational to you. The hair dryer, vacuum cleaner, and dishwasher may have no effect on him, while the sound of your electric toothbrush may send him into fits of terrified crying. He may love the tub, the pool, and sticking his hands in your glass of water but become hysterical if you try to wash his hands under running water in the sink.

Babies like the expected. Anything new or outside their routine has the potential to be scary for them. Even things that baby will eventually love, like swinging on a swing set, might be frightening at first. The more closely you can share new experiences with your baby, the more likely he is to ease into them and enjoy them. You might try swinging together on a grown-up swing first, for instance.

Even if you can't understand what causes baby's fears, it is important that you respect them. After all, most of us have a few irrational fears of our own! The more you can steer baby away from things that frighten him, the better. Don't make a big deal of it—just support and comfort him when he's afraid, and respect the fear enough to help him avoid experiencing it again. Trying to get baby to face the fear and work through it will backfire and only intensify his anxiety. The less often baby is frightened, the faster his fears will disappear.

78.

Don't fall for the old "good for his lungs" line.

Just to put the record straight, your mother-in-law is wrong. Leaving baby to cry alone is not good for baby's lungs or any other part of him. Your lack of attentiveness will cause him to cry much more than he needs to. Unnecessary crying expends an enormous amount of energy and wastes valuable calories. It floods baby's bloodstream with stress hormones. His gut tenses up. His breathing becomes labored and irregular. His heart pounds. His limbs stiffen, and his little facial muscles tense painfully.

Plus, prolonged, unattended crying has a negative effect on sleep patterns, causing the exhausted baby to fall into a deep, unhealthy sleep. It interferes with time that baby could spend happily learning about his world. And, as discussed elsewhere, it can lead to a devastating lack of self-worth and a host of other psychological problems.

Developmental psychologist Sharon Heller, Ph.D., says, "For prolonged crying to be normal and expected for infants, it would have to meet at least two conditions. It would have to be a universal characteristic of infants, which it isn't, and it would have to serve some important survival function, which it doesn't."

No good can come from letting a baby cry unattended. Mothers who routinely ignore their babies' cries—even for brief periods—are at risk for becoming so tuned out that they fail to recognize cries that signal pain or illness and thereby neglect meeting their babies' medical needs.

Listening to a baby crying is so grating on the nerves that it can even cause a parent to feel anger toward the baby. The last thing a crying baby needs is an angry caregiver. Babies cannot be fooled by fake smiles or insincere warmth. They are born with an extremely high sensitivity to signs of hostility or withdrawal, particularly from their parents. This is part of their hardwiring, because their very survival depends on loving care from others.

79.

Make baby smart while you make him happy.

Infancy represents a mere 2 percent of our lifespans, yet 80 percent of brain growth occurs within the first two years of life. How much baby's brain grows is directly proportional to how much stimulation it gets. Every experience baby has is an opportunity for learning. Babies are born craving experience, with an innate drive to learn as much as they can.

When you make baby a part of your life, especially when you carry baby through his infancy, think of the richness he gets access to! It's true that babies can be overstimulated, but if baby is comfy in a sling against your body, he'll just hunker down and go to sleep when he's had enough learning for the moment.

Every sight, every sound, every smell, and every object you let baby explore fires off neurons in baby's brain that branch out and grow, creating new neurons. Offering baby a constant flow of sensory input not only makes him happy, it also makes him smart!

And it's surprisingly simple to keep baby stimulated. You don't need special toys or flash cards or anything more than what you normally encounter in your daily life. Just holding baby makes the biggest difference of all. Studies on rats have proved the correlation between touch and brain growth. Baby rats that are frequently touched and petted grow to become smarter rats than ones that are not handled.

Every moment your baby spends in contact with you is a moment he's being stimulated and getting smarter. And every moment he spends alone in a container is a precious opportunity that's lost forever.

80.

Skip the "loveys."

"Loveys" are the security blankets, tattered stuffed animals, or other objects that so many children form strong attachments to. Many magazine articles and some books claim that attachment to a lovey, or transitional object, is a healthy stage in breaking away from dependence on a parent. Some even recommend supplying such an object when attempting to crib-train a baby.

But the experts on the other side of the fence warn that, while common, there is nothing healthy about fixating on an inanimate object for comfort and companionship. Children who are weaned from their parents' arms before they are ready take comfort in whatever parent substitute is available.

Psychologically, of course, the substitution is a poor one. In a very obvious way, it trains the child to bond to things instead of to people. As the child matures, he may seek out bigger and more expensive material possessions to try to fill the void his early lack of parenting left in him. But things can never fill that void.

Babies who are brought up attachment-parenting-style don't form attachments to loveys—they form attachments to parents. Dr. William Sears explains: "The infant who is accustomed to being in arms, at breast, and in mommy and daddy's bed receives security and fulfillment from personal relationships. This infant is more likely to become a child who forms meaningful attachments with peers and in adulthood is more likely to develop a deep intimacy with a mate. The child who is often left by himself in swings, cribs, and playpens is at risk for developing shallow interpersonal relationships and becoming increasingly unfulfilled by a materialistic world."

81.

Don't underestimate the value of dad!

Dads are totally undervalued in our society. The influence of a close relationship with Dad throughout a child's development has been proved to be completely necessary for optimal development of both girls and boys. Jails are full of fatherless boys who got into trouble while struggling to develop their masculinity without the help of a positive male role model.

Baby expert Tine Thevenin says that working in combination, the separate roles of each parent contribute what's necessary for optimum child rearing. While mothers are typically nurturers who make a child feel safe and unconditionally accepted, it is fathers who encourage their children to do their best, stretch their limits, and succeed in achieving their goals. The two types of parenting complement one another to create the perfect balance, whereas too much of either upsets the balance.

Luckily, dads are rising to the occasion! According to Michael Lamb, Ph.D., in his book, *The Role of the Father in Child Development,* recent studies have shown that dads today are spending 33 percent more time with their kids than dads did twenty years ago. That means that men are spending an average of two to three hours a day engaged with their children.

The period immediately following the birth of a child can be hard on a Dad, though. He doesn't have the same automatic physical connection a mom does with the new family member, and he's likely to be frustrated if Mom becomes completely preoccupied with baby, leaving him feeling like the odd man out.

In her excellent guide, *The Pregnancy Sourcebook,* M. Sara Rosenthal writes, "We now know that a significant number of new fathers experience depression. Like women, men who don't feel ready for a new baby or who have lower self-esteem are more at risk for depression. In addition, men who have unresolved conflicts with their own fathers are also prone to psychological problems or depression when becoming fathers themselves."

It's a wise investment of your time to make sure your husband feels appreciated for all the sacrifices he's making and the efforts he's putting forth for you and the baby. Most of all, resist the urge to believe that you are uniquely designed to best meet all of baby's needs. Your husband needs time to develop his own bond with baby, in his own way. Both he and baby will benefit greatly from these early bonding efforts.

Many Dads of breastfed babies worry that they can't compete for baby's affection because Mom has the market cornered on nourishing her. But studies have proved that cuddling and plentiful skin-to-skin contact have a much greater impact on bonding than feeding does. In a famous experiment in the 1950s with rhesus monkeys, infant-researcher Harry Harlow proved that touch is a more powerful bonding tool than is sustenance.

Harlow separated monkey infants from their mothers and built them instead two inanimate surrogate mothers. One, made out of terry cloth and heated from the inside with a lightbulb, was soft and warm. The other, made of hard wire, had a bottle attached to it from which the monkeys received their nourishment. The baby monkeys spent only as much time with the wire mother as they needed to ensure proper nutrition for themselves, but up to twenty-two hours a day they clung to the terry-cloth mother!

When left alone with each surrogate separately, the monkeys showed some signs of attachment to the terry-cloth mom but none at all to the wire one. These results clearly demonstrated that the "mother" monkey who *felt* more nurturing was preferred to the one who delivered the goods! (These monkeys didn't fare well in the long run, by the way. Having been deprived of genuine contact with a live parent, they grew up neurotic, asocial, and sexually inept.)

It's loving touch that makes a lifelong difference in infants—monkey or human—and dads are just as well equipped to provide this as moms are.

82.

Don't be a "no" machine!

Most crawlers and newly toddling toddlers have a habit of singling out—and pouncing on—the very most off-limit thing in any room. Maddening as it is, try to think of this tendency as a healthy addiction. Your baby truly cannot help himself. If he didn't have this intense curiosity, he wouldn't learn things at the amazing rate that is normal for his age. And if he didn't strongly object to your interference with his learning, he wouldn't have the determination to persist when faced with life's little setbacks.

For a parent to avoid becoming a "no" machine requires diligence and creativity. When baby must be stopped in his tracks, alternatives like "Stop!" or calling baby's name in just the right tone of voice can be more effective than the standard "No!" My friend Kim hated overhearing mothers trying to discipline their kids in public, so she worked out a code with her eighteen-month-old, Christopher.

Whenever he was headed for trouble, a sharp "Ahhh!" from Kim would literally freeze him in place until she got a chance to redirect his behavior.

No matter what word you use at the moment of impending disaster, you'll need to follow it up with a distraction of some kind in order to avoid a major upset for your child. You know your baby best, so keep a mental list of the things he loves. That way you can always redirect his attention to a favorite activity, song, or toy. If Tuck and I were anywhere near any light switch, I could always woo him away from a no-no by saying, "Tucker turn on the light?" He would nod enthusiastically and hold up his arms for me to carry him to the light switch where I would cheer wildly at his expert manipulation of it.

After the first year, babies recognize a lot of words, even if they can't say them yet. Dr. William Sears recommends using the word for the distraction as the word to stop baby. He says, "One pattern of association we noted in Matthew's developmental diary was that when I would say 'Go' to sixteen-month-old Matthew he would get the baby sling and run to the door. We used this ability to associate for distraction discipline: When we saw Matthew headed for major mischief we'd say 'Go.' This cue was enough to motivate his mind and body to change direction. We filed away a list of cue words to use as 'redirectors' ('ball,' 'cat,' 'go,' and so on). Of course, you must carry through and go for a walk or play ball or find the cat; otherwise your child will come to distrust you and you will lose a useful discipline tool."

Remember when using any discipline technique that your child will only learn what's off-limits and what's not if you are consistent. And expect to be consistent for a long time. Most babies don't fully develop the cognitive ability to remember and act upon prior instructions until they are at least two years old.

83.

Know when to encourage and when to rescue.

Your toddler will come across lots of dilemmas while practicing all those fabulous new skills that come with toddlerdom. She may throw a ball farther than she intended and be unsure how to extract it from beneath the sofa. She may become wedged between a chair and an ottoman. She may want to navigate her wagon through a particularly challenging course around the kitchen island and into the family room but become frustrated when the trip doesn't go smoothly.

When a loving parent witnesses any of these events, the natural inclination is to rush to the rescue. Instead, size up the problem first. Is it one she could handle alone? If so, try encouraging her verbally. "Emily do it" may be all she needs to increase her confidence in her own abilities. Then, if she successfully gets past the difficulty on her own, what a boost to her self-esteem! If she doesn't, by all means help her, but try to do so in a way that lets her feel at least partly responsible for the success. Say, "Mommy will help Emily," not "Mommy will do it for Emily."

84.

Be a good boo-boo fixer.

When your toddler starts suffering boo-boos, your reactions to his little injuries will go a long way toward shaping his feelings about himself, his body, and how he will handle life's setbacks. Take your cues from him! If you rush in with a worried voice and face every time he stumbles, he will think himself fragile and the world a dangerous place. If you go to the other extreme and answer his cries coolly with statements like "Oh, that didn't hurt you!" or "Don't be a baby. It's not that bad," he will learn that you discount his feelings. He may even get the message that his feelings annoy you and so begin stifling them. And, imitating your behavior, he will later be insensitive to other people's problems.

I love Dr. William Sears's description of how his wife, Martha, matches the child's emotions with her own:

> Instead of locking into her own adult mind, she would click into the child's view of the problem. She would first match the child's emotional state. If the child's emotions registered a '10' on the boo-boo rating scale, Martha's empathy would rate a '10.' She was using the oldest negotiating trick in the world: First, meet people where they are, and then carry them where you want them to be. Martha would gradually begin lessening her worry signals, which would help the child wind down into the realization that the scrape was not the end of his life. He would realize that if the hurt was no big deal in Mommy's eyes, it was not worth wasting energy on, and he would go back to his play, happily sporting a Band-Aid.

Little bandages can deliver great psychological healing powers by reassuring toddlers that their pain is being recognized and that something concrete is being done to help. Alice Sterling Honig, Ph.D., professor of child development at Syracuse University, says in *Parents* magazine, "Keep two kinds of bandages on hand. By giving children a choice, you're giving them power—which is exactly what they need when they're feeling vulnerable." (She also warns that adhesive bandages can be dangerous choking hazards for children under five years old and advises removing the bandage if you see your child sucking on it.)

Of course, if your toddler is lucky enough to still be nursing, you have access to the oldest and best boo-boo fixer there is. Breastfeeding moms have a reliable means of determining whether a boo-boo is serious or not because their babies are so consistently comforted by nursing. Whether it's a scrape, a bump, a bruise, or just bruised feelings, nursing instantly stops the crying and starts the mending. If it doesn't, they know the boo-boo's major.

85.

Give your toddler an adult view of her world.

Toddlers love nothing more than to be included in your adult world. But little hands reaching into your cooking, cleaning, or hobbying can be dangerous and inconvenient. My friend Holly solved the problem beautifully with her daughter, Taylor, by buying a lightweight, steel-frame backpack.

Taylor adores her perch on Mommy's back, looking over Holly's shoulder with a ringside view of all those fascinating things mommy does. Most parents utilize backpacks solely for outdoor excursions, but around the house they come in handy for accomplishing tasks without excluding baby.

The sling provides the perfect place for an infant to observe Mommy's doings. But the sling is not as ideal around the house with a toddler unless she is tired and wants to fall asleep against a loving parent. (The sling is still perfect for toting toddlers on outings, though!) In their homes, toddlers generally like to get around on their own, but if Mommy is involved in something that interests them, they will want to watch. The backpack is a great perch for them to watch from because its height is inherently exciting and it also keeps little hands an appropriate distance from the activity!

I visited Holly's home the other day and found her sitting at her table, giving a friend a manicure, with Taylor watching intently from above. One caveat: Holly warns against letting your toddler snack while in the backpack unless you want to experiment with gooey globs of partially chewed banana as a hair conditioner.

86.

Be flexible, even with your "nos."

When you tell your toddler "no" in a new situation and he cries and you decide to let him do/have/touch whatever it was he was after, you will undoubtedly get some raised eyebrows from grandparents or neighbors who have warned you not to let baby "get the upper hand." Ignore them. There are battles that are worth waging and those that are not. Filling your child's world with unnecessary restrictions will not make him a better-behaved child; it will just make him a bored, unhappy one.

A child doesn't protest a "no" in order to gain control over you personally—it's his world and his environment he's trying to gain control over, and that's a healthy part of growing up. His protest is just his way of letting you know he really, really wants something.
If it's something you can tolerate, show him that you're willing to be flexible and make him happy whenever possible.

Often, the "no" will need to be a firm one, of course. This is espeically the case if you've said "no" before and are reinforcing the message with your consistent response. When the "no" is non-negotiable, calmly make that clear on the very first signs of protest—and do not waver. If he knows you'll bend for him when you can, he'll be more likely to back down and accept your dictates when they're absolute. Only if you frequently back down even from your firm "nos" will he get the message that wailing will convince you to change your mind.

87.

Indulge your toddler's obsessions.

Around the time your baby starts talking you may be surprised to find that she has definite preferences among all the things she's learned to label. Your baby naturally loves to master new things, and by focusing in on one particular area of interest, she can more easily master a subject than if she'd scattered her concentration among a great variety of things.

Maybe your baby has decided that dogs are her passion and she's become an expert at pointing out dogs wherever you go. She sees them not only in the neighborhood, but in books, in wallpaper at the pediatrician's office, on television, on boxes at the grocery store, and on her clothes. She barks and growls enthusiastically and may even deem horses, hippos, and any other four-legged creatures dogs as well. She will tirelessly point out dogs' tails, noses, paws, and ears for you and will love toy dogs above all other toys.

As bored as *you* are becoming with dogs, suppress your urge to direct baby's attention to broader horizons. In a bewildering world that offers a continual flow of new information to process, a familiar object of delight is a welcome reprieve! Trying to assimilate a lot of new stuff, your baby can say to herself, "Hey, there's something I know about! Let's talk about that for a while!" Indulging her enthusiasm for her favorite topics will increase baby's self-esteem and make her even more interested in mastering new subjects to add to her repertoire.

Let baby direct his own play.

For us grown-ups, play is extra. It's what we get to do when the work is done. But for your baby, play is a very important and exhausting job. It's the means by which baby learns the different properties of the things around him; how they feel, what happens when he drops them or moves them in certain ways, how to control his body in order to manipulate them, how to interact with them. Babies are instinctively driven to explore and learn. It may look like frivolous fun to us, but to baby it's another day hard at work! And since play satisfies their need for intellectual stimulation, babies enjoy it immensely and have a great time doing it. Don't you envy the little laborers?

Even when you've just brought home what you consider to be a fabulous toy, temper your urge to direct baby's play. Your baby knows exactly what the best toy for him is at any given time, and often it will be one that has never before carried the label "toy." The best way you can help baby with his job is to observe him closely and give him the opportunity to play with the things that interest him.

Not surprisingly, babies often will choose things they see you "playing with" over the toys you provide solely for their amusement. Few babies can resist pots and pans and a spatula for banging. Other household favorites include a remote control with the batteries out, all shapes and sizes of food storage containers, measuring spoons, an unplugged or de-batteried telephone, wooden kitchen utensils, colanders, key rings, ice cube trays, cassette tape boxes, whisks, funnels, pieces of tape, or even small, interesting objects secured in sealed, unbreakable plastic bags.

Before you throw anything away, try to see it from baby's eyes. Would it make a great new toy for a few hours? Strewn amidst the pricey stuff in Tucker's toy boxes were often emptied (and washed) yogurt containers, egg cartons, plastic bottles, toilet paper tubes, odd socks, big and small boxes, plastic cups, and other junk that he loved even more than grandma's latest installment from FAO Schwarz mail order.

89.

Ride your toddler's dependency roller coaster with him.

Toddlers are confused and confusing little creatures. One moment they're clinging to you like lint on wool and the next, you can't catch them. This is completely appropriate toddler behavior! Your little explorer is relishing his newfound independence, but the more he realizes he can do without you, the more he needs to make sure he still has access to you.

You are the secure base from which he can venture forth, and only by striking a balance between the security of you and the thrill of independence will he be happy. Think of your toddler as a battery-operated being and yourself as the battery charger. The time he spends wrapped affectionately in your arms provides an emotional recharging that enables him to enjoy time away from you. Let him be the judge of how much time he needs with and without you, and he'll always get just the right amount.

This roller coaster works on two levels. It operates within any given hour (or minute!) and it also works on a larger scale, from month to month. Dr. William Sears describes it like this: "The same child who spent two months in a snit may act like an angel for the next three. This developmental quirk can work to a child's advantage and to yours. Spot which phase your child is in. If he's trying to move away and grow up a bit, let out the line. During this phase, your child may seem distant from you; he may even answer back and defy you. Don't take this personally. This phase will soon pass. The child is just in the 'do it myself' phase and needs some space and coaching (including correcting) from the sidelines. One day soon, as sure as sunrise follows nightfall, you'll find your child snuggling next to you on the couch." Rest assured, your toddler's alternate disconnecting and reconnecting is healthy and as long as you are expecting it, you can make an effort to stay in harmony with his needs.

90.

Respect your baby's wishes, even when they conflict with yours.

When you want your older baby to do something and she wants to do the opposite, how you handle your request can greatly affect its success. Remember, baby learns behavior by watching you. Respect for the other guy's feelings is the cornerstone of discipline. And if you expect your baby to respect your feelings, you've got to respect hers.

Suppose you want to get baby in the car for a trip to the grocery store, but she's playing happily on the floor and doesn't want to be removed from her toys. Do you really have to leave for the store right at that moment? If you explain to baby that you need for you and her to go to the store, but you will wait a little longer until she is ready, she will learn that you value and respect her wishes. The following day, your departure time may not be negotiable, but baby will be less likely to put up a fuss because she has learned from you to respect the wishes of people she loves.

91.

Meet toddler defiance with age-appropriate discipline.

The very same natural tendencies that cause your toddler to defy you are the ones that will help him to succeed as he matures. Life would be easier for parents if babies were compliant little creatures who never disagreed with them, but it wouldn't be healthy for the babies themselves.

Without a very strong sense of determination, baby would never master all of the difficult developmental milestones ahead of him.

That doesn't mean you should give into baby's every wish or condone his defiant behavior. But understanding it will help you to deal with it better. The key to effective discipline is repetition. You must decide what the rules are and be very persistent in enforcing them. And don't be angry or frustrated when you have to teach the rules over and over and over again. Babies don't have great memories, and only through LOTS of repetition will they learn.

When you need to discipline your toddler, don't do it haphazardly. Have a set pattern you follow that your child will come to recognize, and make sure your tone is respectful. Use his name, look him directly in the eye, and state your rule as simply as possible. Don't smile, but don't show anger either. You manner should be authoritative and matter-of-fact. Physically remove your child from the no-no situation, or remove the forbidden object from his hand. Then substitute an acceptable activity or object, resume your friendly attitude, and put the incident behind you. Harping on his misbehavior will have no corrective effect at this age and will only up your stress.

Hopefully, you already know this, but DON'T SPANK YOUR BABY! Remember, your baby isn't the enemy. If he persists with an undesirable activity even after you have used your most authoritative tone of voice, he likely does not understand or is simply too intent on the activity to be able to stop himself. Remove him from the activity calmly and without a big fuss. Then, when he is no longer engaged in the activity, give him lots of hugs and praises.

Make sure your actions and words clearly convey the message that you dislike the thing he is doing but that you love *him* always and unconditionally. You will know when your baby is capable of understanding the reasons he can't do certain things. Once that understanding kicks in, you can begin explaining why certain behavior is not acceptable. This will start him on the long but rewarding road to self-discipline.

Hopefully, you already know this but DON'T SPANK YOUR BABY! Almost all child development specialists now agree that physical punishment is an ineffective discipline tool. Plus, when you hurt a child, you teach him that violence is an acceptable way to solve conflicts. Remember, your baby isn't the enemy?

92.

Tone down tantrums.

Some time after baby's first birthday, you may start to recognize some crying bouts as true tantrums: those explosions of frustrated feelings resulting from him wanting to do much more than he is capable of doing and not having the language skills to release his frustrations in any other way.

All children go through a tantrum stage, but some have worse tantrums than others and some children's stages last longer than others. According to Kathy Levinson, Ph.D., author of *First Aid for Tantrums*, 14 percent of one-year-olds have tantrums every day, while 20 percent of two- and three-year-olds have two or more tantrums per day. Tantrums are natural expressions of strong, bottled-up emotions that come with the territory of being a toddler. Even attachment-parented babies with very secure bonds to their caregivers will, at some point, become frustrated with their own limitations or the limitations their caregivers impose on them.

It's natural for your baby to cry when you take away a dangerous object or say no to a forbidden activity. He doesn't like the turn of events and he's letting you know that. Give voice to his distress by empathetically naming the problem for him. "I know you wanted to play with Daddy's electric drill. It's hard when you see Daddy using something and you can't share it. Let's read a book instead!"

If your cheerful attempt at distraction fails and your child proceeds with a full-blown angry protest, he probably needs to release stress through crying. Don't yell or act disapprovingly toward him; you will only compound his misery. He'll be much better able to calm down if you yourself remain calm.

In their excellent guide, *The Discipline Book*, William and Martha Sears say, "Tantrums are due to frustration (your toddler is trying a complicated engineering feat and howls when it goes wrong), so don't ignore this need for help. Take this tantrum as an opportunity to connect: By helping your child out of a tight spot, you build authority and trust. Offer a helping hand, a comforting 'It's okay,' and direct his efforts toward a more manageable part of the task (for example, you slip the sock halfway onto the foot, and then he can pull it on all the way)."

If that doesn't help, the Searses recommend holding the tantruming toddler in a loving embrace: "Your strong arms in place around him give the message that since he's out of control you have stepped in to help him hold himself together. You may or may not be heard, but you can speak softly near his ear reassuring phrases like 'Mama's here. I'll help you. Show me what you need,' and so on."

Once baby has calmed down, try nursing or offering a nutritious snack. Tantrums often take place when baby is hungry or tired. Look for patterns in the conditions surrounding baby's tantrums so that you can try to circumvent them.

Some experts advise ignoring or punishing tantrums but doing this will only tell baby that he is not entitled to have these feelings. Children need your loving guidance to help them deal with the scariness of their out-of-control emotions. They also need you to set reasonable limits for them and to be consistent in enforcing those limits. Never reverse a decision based on a tantrum. When baby is raging over not being given a third cookie and you decide mid-tantrum to fork up the cookie, you're not only sending a bad message, but you're denying him the opportunity to release his frustrations through crying.

93.

Mellow out a little aggressor.

Around the same time that tantruming surfaces, many toddlers also go through a phase of acting aggressively toward others. Like tantrums, aggressive behaviors are usually the result of frustrations that babies are unable to verbalize. William and Martha Sears say, "Toddlers become aggressive in order to release pent-up anger, to control a situation, to show power, or to protect their turf in a toy squabble. Some children even resort to obnoxious behavior in a desperate attempt to break through to distant parents."

My friend Joy successfully remedied aggression in eighteen-month-old Zoe with this approach. Whenever Zoe hit or bit another child, Joy would pick her up, remove her from the play scene and, with a serious look on her face, firmly say "No hitting," or "No biting." She would sit away from the others with Zoe on her lap, facing away from her, for a slow count to ten. Zoe would be squirming to get down to return to the toys and other babies, but Joy would hold her firmly in place without talking to her.

After the ten seconds, she would happily take Zoe back to the group, sit down with her, and model friendly play with the other children. Joy says it took a while, but once Zoe figured out that every aggressive action she took was going to result in removal from the fun, she curbed her biting and hitting tendencies.

Sometimes parents are on the receiving end of babies' aggressive moves. The Searses suggest redirecting experimental slapping into a game of "Give me five" and responding to biting by saying firmly, "No biting. Ouchie. Hurts Mama!" and then redirecting the behavior with a happier expression, saying, "Hug Mama. That's nice!"

If baby hits, bites, or kicks a parent out of anger, the Searses advise the following approach: "Firmly but calmly announce 'You may not hit' and put her down . . . Give her the message that you will not let her hurt you. If you don't allow your child to hurt you when he's very young, he will be less likely to let others hurt him when he's older. You will be modeling to him how to say no to being hit by, for example, holding up a hand to stop the blow but not hitting back."

Since baby is still likely to be angry over whatever the problem was, try putting his anger into words for him: "I know you are feeling angry that you had to return your cousin's toy, but you may not hurt people." Aggressive actions won't go away without parental intervention, so take the necessary steps to curb these behaviors as soon as they appear.

94.

Show your toddler how to give and receive help.

Toddlers need a lot of help doing things. But as they start to become independent little people, they want to do many of those things themselves. Be sensitive to your child's desires for help or independence. Whenever possible, let your child decide whether or not to go it alone. If you deny your baby your help when she asks for it, or if you insist on giving it when it's not wanted, she will form unhealthy associations with the concept of helping. You probably know a few adults with this problem—the ones who won't accept help from anyone or, on the other hand, those who rely too heavily on help from others.

When your baby is old enough to understand, start asking for *her* help in doing things. Children love to help their parents. It makes them feel important and needed and demonstrates that helping one another is what loved ones do. Among Tuck's favorite "helping" activities were laundry sorting, sweeping, unloading the dishwasher, bed making, putting away groceries after shopping, dusting everything he could reach with his own dust cloth, and brushing Mama's hair.

95.

Share laughs with baby.

Your baby's sense of humor may start to develop near his first birthday. Babies laugh from the time they're about four months old, but those early laughs are usually in response to joyful feelings or pleasant physical sensations rather than in reaction to something that strikes them as funny. Since one-year-olds have some experience with how things are supposed to be, incongruities can crack them up. (Our Uncle Gerry gets big laughs by wearing Tuck's socks on his ears.)

There is nothing in life so absolutely delicious as a baby's belly laugh. Every time I find something new that cracks up Tucker I simply cannot stop myself from cracking up with him—or from repeating the thing unflaggingly. And it's almost impossible for two people to share laughter and not feel a heightened degree of bonding!

I'll never forget the first joke Tucker made all by himself at fourteen months. He knew the answer to the question, "What's your name?" and had been proudly sharing this for several weeks with strangers in checkout lines. But one day, when I asked him the same question, he glanced with devilishly twinkling eyes over at my husband and answered, "Dada!" and then dissolved into laughter. There was no mistaking the intention—this wasn't a lapse of memory or an identity crisis. It was a joke! It was so darn cute that my husband and I laughed quite a bit over it, which Tucker loved. In fact, he loved it so much that for the next four weeks, the answer to "What's your name?" was a gleefully uttered "Dada" every time.

Sharing laughter with your baby is not only a tremendous bonding tool, it's really healthy too! According to Annette Goodheart, Ph.D., author of *Laughter Therapy*, laughter actually strengthens the immune system, enhances cardiovascular flexibility, increases intellectual performance and information retention, and rebalances the chemistry of stress hormones in your body. To think that you can do all that for yourself and your baby just by having a lot of fun!

My friend Julie accidentally stumbled on a way to get laughs out of her baby, Luke, when Luke decided one day that the sound of her sniffing his diaper was the most hysterical thing in the world. Initially, she would do the sniff test for obvious practical reasons, but Luke's response turned it into a favorite game. Babies love unusual noises, funny faces, and quick, silly movements. Slapstick pretend falls as well as real falls are likely to get a laugh. When baby laughs at a physical mishap, it's not malicious, since baby is unlikely to realize that the faller is at risk for injury. It's the surprise of the unexpected that baby finds funny.

My friend Reyna makes Tucker laugh uncontrollably by straddling a mop and pretending to ride it, horsey style, all around the house. My mom doubles him over with a gravity-defying dance to the tune of "Jingle Bells" that would make me rich if I relinquished a video of it to one of those home video shows. My husband cracks him up with exaggerated fake hiccups, and all Auntie Cheryl has to do is shake her curly hair at him. Keep a mental list of what makes your baby laugh—tried-and-true giggle getters are great distraction devices for heading off tantrums and undesirable behavior.

By the second half of the second year, verbal jokes are as likely to get a laugh as sight gags are, and you'll soon catch on to your child's favorite funny phrases. According to Parents magazine, "People tend to respond most to jokes that cut closest to their fears and obsessions and toddlers are no different. They prefer jokes about skills they've just mastered—like table etiquette, walking, or speaking correctly—which still carry an emotional charge. Laughter helps release stress and frustration."

96.

Provide plenty of (safe) buttons for baby to push.

Sometime around your baby's first birthday, you may notice that no button in the house is safe from pushing, no knob is safe from turning, no switch is safe from switching. Babies love to imitate their parents, and your toys are likely to attract him much more than his own. Televisions, stereos, phones, car key remotes, computer switches, briefcase closures . . . the list of manipulatives that are irresistible to tiny hands is endless.

One solution a friend of mine discovered is to give the little technician his own grown-up toys—not the plastic, colorful versions made by toy manufacturers, but authentic castoffs found at garage sales or contributed by friends and family members. Any defunct gadget—phone, calculator, computerized address book—can become a treasured possession as baby hones those fine-motor skills.

Whenever feasible, let baby practice on the real, working stuff too. He will love the feeling of power he gets from turning on and off a light switch or fan and witnessing the results. Baby-proof your home to make sure that he doesn't hurt himself or damage anything valuable; then spend some time with him supervising his experiences with the things you decide are fair game for experimentation.

97.

Use baby-friendly strategies to keep baby away from danger.

Keeping baby out of danger is one very common source of conflict between mommies and babies. Babies often seem to seek out the most dangerous situations for their fun. Baby-proofing the home can go a long way toward preempting conflict. The more safe you can make your home, the less you'll have to police baby's activities as she begins to crawl and eventually toddle around the house.

Whenever possible, let baby do whatever it is she's trying to do. If there is a chance she'll get hurt doing it, make sure you're in a position to head off injury. If you carefully supervise but allow baby her thorough investigation of a potentially dangerous situation, you might actually satisfy her curiosity about it, thereby saving yourself countless grueling weeks of the stop-the-baby routine.

When you do have to stop baby from doing what she really wants to do, distract, distract, distract. If she grabs a pair of scissors off your desk, you *could* grab them from her, saying, "No, no, scissors aren't for babies," but this approach is likely to frustrate and anger your little investigator. Instead, quickly substitute a book or ruler or tape dispenser. Talk about the exciting object as you offer it with one hand, and chances are you'll be able to get the scissors away with the other hand without much argument.

There will be times when saying no is unavoidable. Just keep in mind that the less often you say it, the more impact it will have when you do. Most babies can understand "no" by about eight months, and a firmly spoken "no" will usually stop a baby in her tracks. It's the difference in your tone of voice that baby reacts to. That's why "no" works best when used sparingly—if you have established a close, loving bond, baby wants nothing more than to please you. However, if you speak sharply to her on a regular basis, she will soon become immune to your reprimands.

For very dangerous situations such as a toddler running into the street, Martha Sears suggests fully expressing your emotions. Your letting baby know how terrifying her actions are to you will likely convince her that she, too, should be terrified to run into the street. If saved for only the most obviously life-threatening situations, conveying your full-throttle concern to baby will make a lasting impression on her.

98.

Model politeness.

When babies start talking in earnest, around the second half of the second year, they have absolutely no tact. Phrases like "Give me!" or "Do it!" or "That's mine!" are not *meant* to be bossy or demanding. It's just that these simple sentences are the easiest for your young grammarian to say. And when she gets the response she's after by uttering them, her newfound power is so delicious that she's apt to repeat them with increasing enthusiasm.

If you frown or convey the message that her words are inappropriate, you may slow her speech development. Save the etiquette lessons for later! Instead, happily let baby know that she has been understood and repeat her phrase, altering it slightly in a more positive direction. For example, baby says, "Give me juice!" and you cheerfully hand her the cup, saying, "Juice, please? Okay, here is your juice!" Don't use a corrective tone; simply act as though you are repeating her wish. If you tack the word *please* onto all of your requests to her, she'll be more likely to use it for her own requests.

Nonverbal etiquette is best taught by example too. If you forcibly grab things out of your baby's hands, you will teach her to be a grabber. When you need to get something away from baby, hold out your hand and ask for it in a friendly but firm voice. If she refuses to let go, gently pry her fingers off the object while matter-of-factly explaining why she can't have it.

99.

Keep offering the best stress reliever known to babies.

The transition from newborn to preschooler rates as the most stressful a human being ever makes. Even adolescence pales in comparison. The physical and mental upheaval marking these years plays a major role in shaping baby's personality as well as the patterns he follows in dealing with life as he matures. Yet many parents discount babies' emotions during this turbulent period.

Luckily for babies, nature has provided them with an exceedingly healthful, nicely packaged tranquilizer: mommy's breast. I'll mention one last time that nursing's unparalleled nutritional value isn't its only perk. The enormous psychological benefits of nursing are no less wonderful for toddlers than for infants. Don't succumb to our society's pressure to wean your child by a specific calendar date. Only by letting your baby wean according to his own timetable will you take advantage of nursing's benefits package.

And the benefits are substantial. When baby hurts himself, nursing will stop the crying (unless he is seriously injured). When he's overexcited and anxious, nursing will relax him. When he's inexplicably cranky and out of sorts, nursing will comfort and often cheer him up. Babies who are prematurely weaned usually seek comfort from substitutes like pacifiers, thumbs, or blanket corners, but none of these come close to working the magic of the breast.

Mothers who force their babies to wean before the babies are ready reassure themselves that they're simply replacing one source of nourishment for another. However, they are replacing only a fraction of what their babies crave in nursing. The renown psychiatric researcher John Bowlby says of the nutritional and psychological functions of nursing: "Each of these functions is of importance in its own right, and to suppose that nutrition is in some way of primary significance and that attachment is only secondary would be a mistake."

In her excellent guide, *Mothering Your Nursing Toddler,* Norma J. Bumgarner advises:

> The way to achieve a natural weaning if that is your objective is to feed and care for your infant without contrived interferences. Nurse on demand from birth. Forget about other foods until your child asks for them. Then feed your child sensibly, for eating foods other than your milk in the first year usually is more for fun than for nourishment. Except in very hot weather a baby who has begun to ask for other foods does not need, besides your milk, any more liquids than he mooches from your cup or glass. An excellent way to avoid over-feeding or over-watering your baby is to let her do it herself, in her own way, and in her own time.

Bumgarner explains that while some babies will wean naturally before their second birthdays, most do it sometime between the ages of two and four. The child may ask to nurse less and less frequently, or she may just suddenly stop. There is no recognizable pattern. Still, every child will wean herself—when she's ready. Breastfeeding makes mothering easier, not harder. And at no point is it in any way bad for your child or for you. Don't cave into pressure to give up this mutually beneficial and loving aspect of your bond with your child just because you're the last mom on the block still doing it.

100.

Be your baby's biggest fan.

Poor behavior results directly from poor self-esteem. Everyone recognizes the sad lack of self-worth that affects sufferers of child abuse. Thankfully, criminal, prosecutable child abuse is not common. Why then is poor self-image so rampant? It's because abuse doesn't have to be physical or even intense for it to damage a child's fragile, just-emerging sense of self.

Every day, well-intentioned parents make disparaging remarks about their kids, are impatient with them, and hurry them through things that, while seemingly of little value, are important to them. They dismiss their children's interest in or curiosity about anything the parents themselves don't deem worthy of attention. They nag them, discourage them, disrespect them, and treat them in ways they'd never treat other adults.

When anyone—and particularly a child, who is still forming his self-image—is treated in such a way over a long period, he begins to take on the characteristics ascribed to him. He will see himself as his parents seem to: flawed, never fast enough or smart enough or good enough. And then he will become those things. The only way to encourage self-esteem in your child is to value and celebrate him exactly as he is.

Child care expert Tine Thevenin says, "A child whose cries have been answered and whose emotional needs have been met, and who has not been taxed by having to handle feelings of hurt, pain, or fright when she is too young, grows up with a high level of self-esteem. She has been shown that she is worth listening to and being taken seriously. She grows up feeling worthwhile and is unlikely to become an anguished adult forever trying to 'find herself' or defeat an inferiority complex."

101.

Stay in love.

During baby's first two years she grows faster than she ever will again in her entire life. She goes from being a completely helpless, tiny blob with almost no control over her body to a little person who coordinates limbs and brainpower to walk and talk and play and poke and be amazingly different from that lumpy sack you brought home from the hospital.

It is during this teensy-weensy period in her life that baby forms the attitudes, personality traits, and disposition that will be with her forever. Will she start out life liking herself and feeling comfortable with who she is, or doubting herself and lacking trust in the world? To a very great extent, it's up to you. Think of respect as a thing that can be measured in cups. However many cupfuls you give her during these crucial first years is the amount she'll have for herself for all the years to come.

It's no coincidence that the "Do unto others" thing is a big deal in almost every religion around the world. It's the perfect answer to any question that has to do with human interaction. When you have any doubt about how to do right by your baby, ask yourself, "If I were the baby, what would I want my parent to do?"

My friend Kenny tells his toddler, Benjamin, that he's his best friend. I remember my mom using the same words with me when I was a child and how unbelievably special they made me feel. Don't take for granted that your baby will know you love her just because you do. Children need to be *told and shown* every single day how much they are loved.

Adopting the bond-enhancing practices in this book will help you to not just love your child but to *be in love with her.* Think for a moment about how you feel when you fall in love with someone. If you can feel that same level of admiration, connectedness, empathy, and awe for your child, with the same longing to please her and be near her—then you are, without a doubt, raising a happy baby.

Bibliography

Acredolo, Linda, Ph.D., and Susan Goodwyn, Ph.D. *Baby Signs: How to Talk with Your Baby Before Your Baby Can Talk.* Chicago: Contemporary Books, 1996.

American Academy of Child and Adolescent Psychiatry. *Your Child.* New York: HarperCollins, 1998.

Auckett, Amelia D. *Baby Massage: Parent-Child Bonding Through Touch.* New York: Newmarket Press, 1982.

Baldwin, Rahima. *You Are Your Child's First Teacher.* Berkeley, Calif.: Celestial Arts, 1989.

Bowlby, John. *Attachment.* New York: Basic Books, 1969.

————. A Secure Base. *Parent-Child Attachment and Healthy Human Development.* New York: Basic Books, 1988.

Brazelton, T. Berry, M.D. *The Essential Reference: Your Child's Emotional and Behavioral Development.* Reading, Mass: Perseus Books, 1992.

————. *Infants and Mothers: Differences in Development.* New York: Delta/Seymour Lawrence, 1983.

————. *On Becoming a Family: The Growth of Attachment.* New York: Delta/Seymour Lawrence, 1981.

————. *To Listen to a Child: Understanding the Normal Problems of Growing Up.* Reading, Mass: Addison-Wesley, 1984.

Brazelton, T. Berry, M.D., and Bertrand G. Cramer. *Earliest Relationship: Parents, Infants and the Drama of Early Attachment.* Reading, Mass: Addison-Wesley, 1990.

Briggs, Dorothy Corkille. *Your Child's Self-Esteem.* New York: Doubleday, 1970.

Bumgarner, Norma J. *Mothering Your Nursing Toddler.* Schaumburg, Ill.: La Leche League International, 1994.

Campbell, Don. *The Mozart Effect: Tapping the Power of Music to Heal the Body, Strengthen the Mind and Unlock the Creative Spirit.* New York: Avon Books, 1997.

Chopra, Deepak. *The Seven Spiritual Laws for Parents: Guiding Your Children to Success and Fulfillment.* New York: Harmony Books/Crown Publishers, 1997.

Dyer, Wayne W. *What Do You Really Want for Your Children?* New York: Avon Books, 1997.

Eisenberg, Arlene, Heidi E. Murkoff, and Sandee E. Hathaway, B.S.N. *What to Expect the First Year.* New York: Workman Publishing, 1996.

Engeler, Amy. "Why Babies Laugh." *Parents,* May 1998.

Ferber, Richard, M.D. *Solve Your Child's Sleep Problems.* New York: Fireside/Simon & Schuster, 1996.

Fraiberg, Selma H. *Every Child's Birthright: In Defense of Mothering.* New York: Basic Books, 1977.

————. *The Magic Years: Understanding and Handling the Problems of Early Childhood.* New York: Charles Scribner's Sons, 1959.

Gerber, Magda, and Allison Johnson. *Your Self-Confident Baby: How to Encourage Your Child's Natural Abilities—from the Very Start.* New York: John Wiley & Sons, 1998.

Goodheart, Annette, Ph.D. *Laughter Therapy: How to Laugh About Everything in Your Life That Isn't Really Funny.* Santa Barbara, Calif.: Less Stress Press, 1994.

Greenspan, Stanley, M.D., and Nancy Thorndike Greenspan. *First Feelings: Milestones in the Emotional Development of Your Baby and Child.* New York: Penguin, 1985.

Heller, Sharon, Ph.D. *The Vital Touch: How Intimate Contact with Your Baby Leads to Happier, Healthier Development.* New York: Henry Holt, 1997.

Klaus, Marshall H., John H. Kennell, and Phyllis Klaus. *Bonding: Building the Foundation of Secure Attachment and Independence.* Reading, Mass.: Addison-Wesley, 1995.

La Leche League International. *The Womanly Art of Breastfeeding.* New York: Plume/Penguin, 1991.

Laliberte, Richard. "Daddy Love." *Parents*, June 1998.

Leach, Penelope. *Your Baby and Child: From Birth to Age Five.* New York: Alfred A Knopf, 1998.

Leonard, Catherine C. "The Solace of the Rocker" *Mothering*, November/December 1998.

Levinson, Kathy, Ph.D. *First Aid for Tantrums.* Boca Raton, Fla.: Saturn Press, 1998.

Liedloff, Jean. *The Continuum Concept: In Search of Happiness Lost.* Reading, Mass.: Addison Wesley, 1977.

McKenna, James. "Sudden Infant Death Syndrome SIDS: Making Sense of Current Research." *Mothering*, Winter 1996.

Marston, Stephanie. *The Magic of Encouragement: Nurturing Your Child's Self-Esteem.* New York: Pocket Books/Simon and Schuster, 1990.

Montagu, Ashley. *Touching: The Human Significance of the Skin.* New York: Harper & Row, 1986.

Morgan, Elisa, and Carol Kuykendall. *What Every Child Needs: Getting to the Heart of Mothering.* Grand Rapids, Mich.: Zondervan Publishing House, 1997.

Morris, Desmond. *Intimate Behavior: A Zoologist's Classic Study of Human Intimacy.* New York: Random House, 1971.

Nolte, Dorothy Law, and Rachel Harris. *Children Learn What They Live: Parenting to Inspire Values.* New York: Workman Publishing, 1998.

Popper, Adrienne. *Parents Book for the Toddler Years.* New York: Ballantine, 1986.

Rosenthal, M. Sara. *The Pregnancy Sourcebook: Everything You Need to Know.* Los Angeles, Calif.: Lowell House, 1997.

Schneider, Vimala. *Infant Massage: A Handbook for Loving Parents.* New York: Bantam, 1982.

Sears, William, M.D., and Martha Sears, R.N. *The Baby Book: Everything You Need to Know About Your Baby from Birth to Age Two.* Boston: Little, Brown, 1993.

———. *The Discipline Book: Everything You Need to Know to Have a Better-Behaved Child-from Birth to Age Ten.* Boston: Little, Brown, 1995.

———. *Nighttime Parenting: How to Get Your Baby and Child to Sleep.* New York: Penguin, 1987.

Shimm, Patricia Henderson, with Kate Ballen. "Avoiding the Long Goodbye." *Parenting*, September 1998.

Solter, Aletha, Ph.D. *Tears and Tantrums: What to Do When Babies and Children Cry.* Goleta, Calif.: Shining Star Press, 1998.

Spock, Benjamin, M.D. *Dr. Spock's Baby and Child Care.* 7th ed. New York: Dutton/Penguin Putnam, 1998.

Stern, Daniel N. *Diary of a Baby: What Your Child Sees, Feels, and Experiences.* New York: Basic Books, 1990.

———. *The First Relationship: Mother and Infant.* Cambridge, Mass.: Harvard University Press, 1977.

Stoppard, Miriam, M.D. *Complete Baby and Child Care.* New York: Dorling Kindersley, 1998.

Stracher, Cameron. "Bunkmates." *Parents*, April 1998.

Thevenin, Tine. *The Family Bed.* Wayne, N.J.: Avery Publishing Group, 1987.

Tieger, Paul D., and Barbara Barron-Tieger. *Nurture by Nature: Understand Your Child's Personality Type—And Become a Better Parent.* Boston: Little, Brown, 1997.

Verny, Thomas, M.D., with John Kelly. *The Secret Life of the Unborn Child.* New York: Dell Publishing, 1981.

White, Burton L. *The New First Three Years of Life.* New York: Fireside/Simon and Schuster, 1998.

———. *Raising a Happy, Unspoiled Child.* New York: Fireside/Simon and Schuster, 1994.

Willis, Kay, and Maryann Bucknum Brinley. *Are We Having Fun Yet? The 16 Secrets of Happy Parenting.* New York: Warner Books, 1997.

Ziglar, Zig. *Raising Positive Kids in a Negative World.* New York: Ballantine, 1989.

Index